Published by P
Paragon House
Bournemouth,
Tel: 01202 2999
Fax: 01202 2999
http://www.parag

Trouble Shooter! - Hundred
© 1999 RDT Ltd.
© 1999 Paragon Publishing

British Library Cataloguing-in-Publication-Data
A catalogue for this book is available from the British Library

ISBN 1-84179-020-6

While every effort has been made to ensure that the
information contained in **Trouble Shooter! -
Hundreds of PC Tips and Tricks** is accurate, Paragon
Publishing Ltd makes no warranty, either expressed or
implied, as to its quality, performance, merchantability
or fitness for any purpose. Due to the dynamic nature
of the software, Paragon Publishing Ltd cannot
guarantee that the answers to the questions will be
suitable for all versions of the Windows operating
system or any other software mentioned in this book.

Trouble Shooter! - Hundreds of PC Tips and Tricks
is published by Paragon Publishing Ltd, an
independent publishing company. This book is not
published, authorised by, or endorsed, or associated in
any way with Microsoft or any associate or affiliate
company.

Editor: John Taylor
Contributors: Graham Taylor, Rex Last
Design: Jonathan Coates
Printed by: Caledonian International Book Manufacturing Ltd, Glasgow
Published by: Paragon Publishing Ltd

CONTENTS

$e = mc^2$

TROUBLESHOOTING WINDOWS

Windows' Troubleshooting feature provides you with detailed support for the most common problems you might encounter on your computer.

If you're experiencing a problem with your PC that you can't find an answer to in any manual or magazine, you may find it useful to ask the computer itself by way of the Windows Help Troubleshooting feature. The Windows 98 Troubleshooters contained within this can help you quickly diagnose and solve technical problems, offering explanations and making suggestions as to the best course of action. By moving the Help window to one side of the screen you can even keep the instructions in front of you while you follow them, rather than having to print them out first.

WINDOWS TROUBLESHOOTING BOOK

The Troubleshooting book contains help pages on most of the problems that you might encounter on your computer, from difficulty with shutting down to trouble with Internet connections, and covers a wide range of potential problems within each topic. It also gives clear and detailed instructions as to how to go about troubleshooting which, provided that you follow them carefully, should help you to solve your problems with ease. If you can't find the answer you're looking for within the Troubleshooting pages, you can use the direct link to Microsoft's Online Support pages to look for it there.

TOP TIP!

You can access the Help feature, which contains the Troubleshooting book, from nearly all Windows applications by pressing F1 on the keyboard. However, different programs have different Help formats.

WINDOWS TROUBLESHOOTING

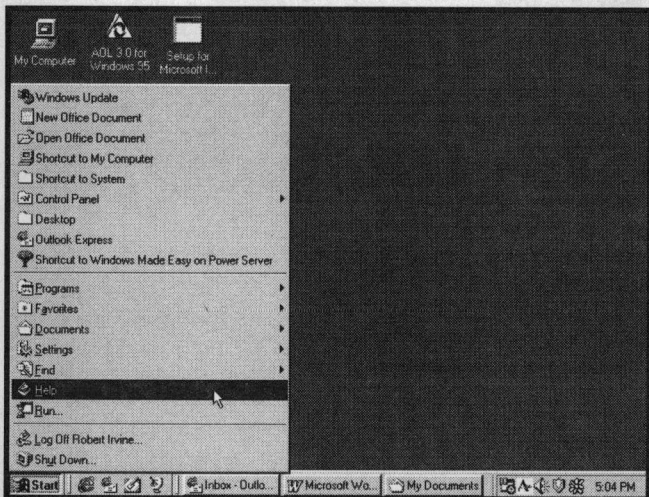

Step 1

To begin, left click the START button and move the mouse pointer up to HELP. Click the left mouse button and the WINDOWS HELP box will now appear onscreen.

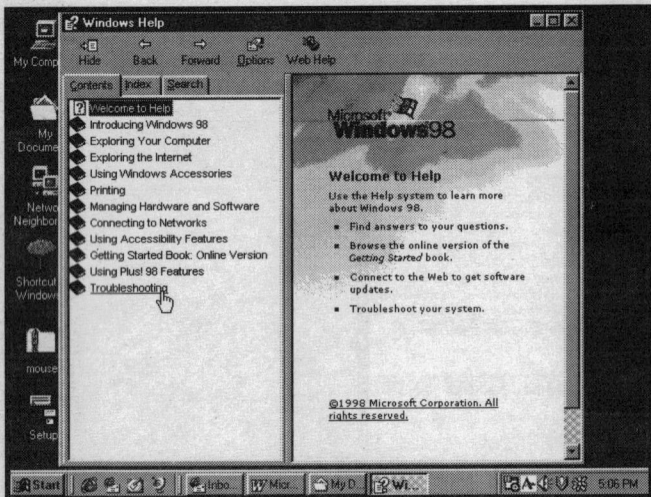

Step 2

Left click on the Windows Help Contents tab. A list of help categories will be displayed on the left-hand side of the screen. Left click on the TROUBLESHOOTING book to open it.

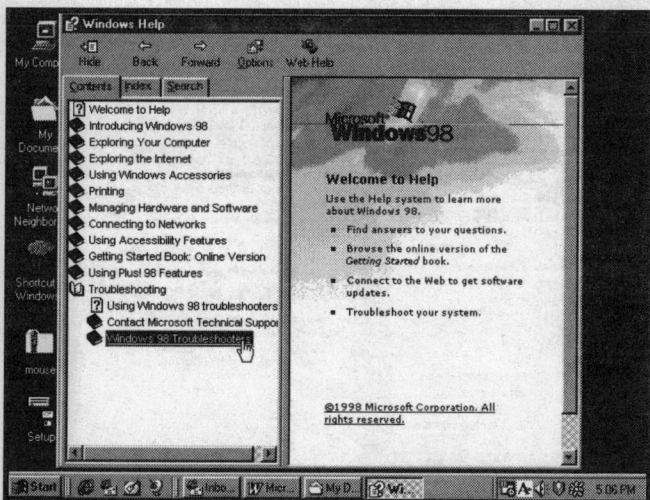

Step 3

A list of further Troubleshooting categories and topics will be displayed. Left click on the Windows 98 Troubleshooters book to list all the TOPICS contained within that category.

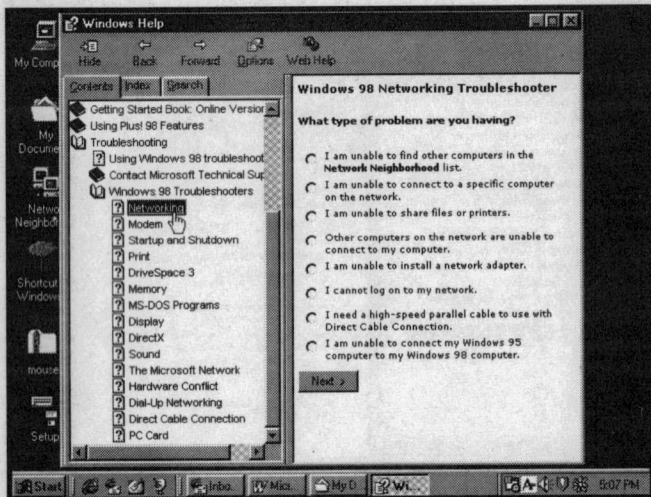

Step 4

Left click on the relevant topic and some TEXT will appear in the right-hand area, asking you what type of problem you are having and listing a number of options to choose from.

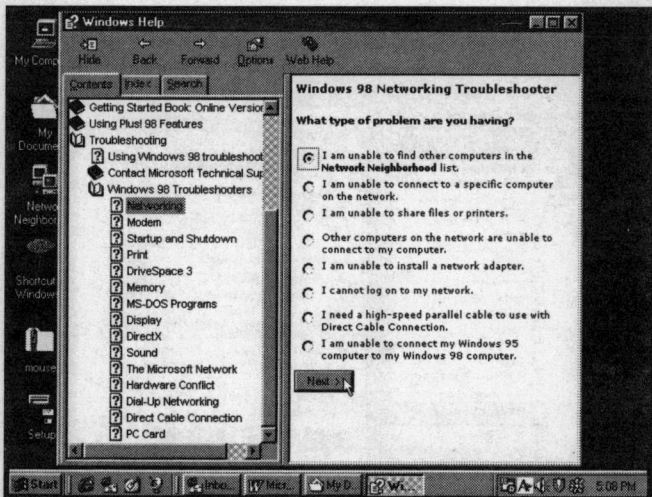

Step 5

Read through the list of options and select the one that best corresponds with your particular problem by left clicking the box to the left of it. Click the NEXT button to continue.

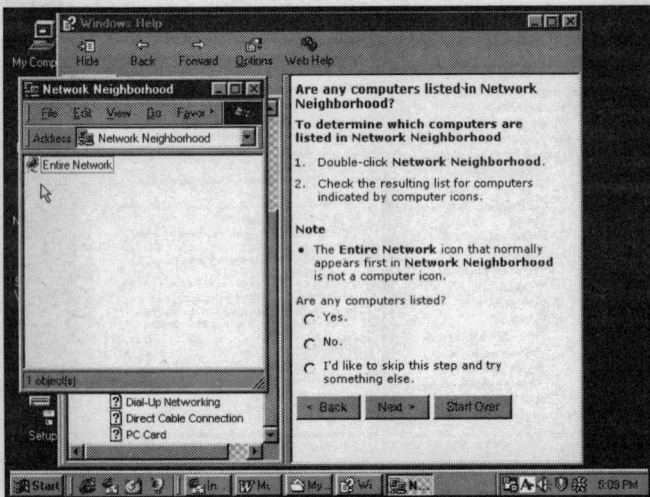

Step 6

The TROUBLESHOOTER will then ask further questions and offer suggestions to help you narrow the problem down. Follow the step-by-step instructions to try this advice out.

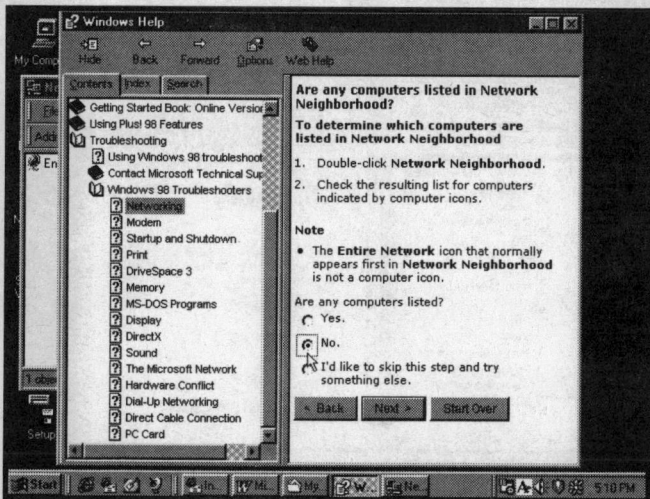

Windows Help

Hide | Back | Forward | Options | Web Help

Contents | Index | Search

- Getting Started Book: Online Version
- Using Plus! 98 Features
- Troubleshooting
  - Using Windows 98 troubleshoot
  - Contact Microsoft Technical Sup
  - Windows 98 Troubleshooters
    - Networking
    - Modem
    - Startup and Shutdown
    - Print
    - DriveSpace 3
    - Memory
    - MS-DOS Programs
    - Display
    - DirectX
    - Sound
    - The Microsoft Network
    - Hardware Conflict
    - Dial-Up Networking
    - Direct Cable Connection
    - PC Card

Are any computers listed in Network Neighborhood?

To determine which computers are listed in Network Neighborhood

1. Double-click **Network Neighborhood**.

2. Check the resulting list for computers indicated by computer icons.

Note

- The **Entire Network** icon that normally appears first in **Network Neighborhood** is not a computer icon.

Are any computers listed?

○ Yes.

◉ No.

○ I'd like to skip this step and try something else.

« Back | Next » | Start Over

Start | ... | 5:10 PM

Step 7

The troubleshooter will ask you whether or not the action solved the problem. Left click the relevant option to reply Yes or No, or alternatively to skip that **SUGGESTION** and try something different.

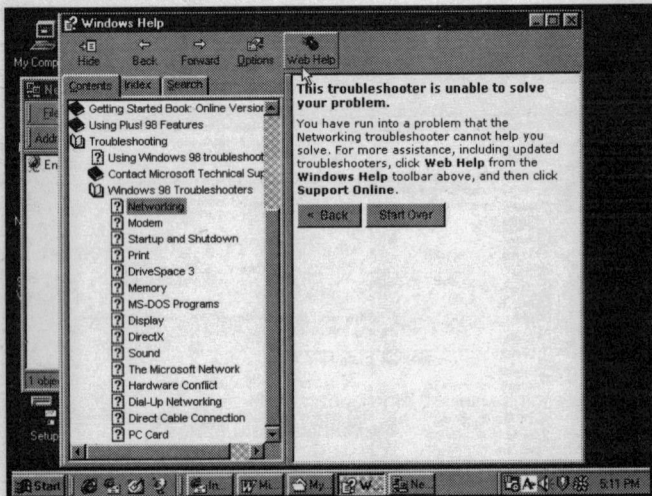

Windows Help

Hide | Back | Forward | Options | Web Help

Contents | Index | Search

- Getting Started Book: Online Version
- Using Plus! 98 Features
- Troubleshooting
  - ? Using Windows 98 troubleshoot
  - Contact Microsoft Technical Sup
  - Windows 98 Troubleshooters
    - ? Networking
    - ? Modem
    - ? Startup and Shutdown
    - ? Print
    - ? DriveSpace 3
    - ? Memory
    - ? MS-DOS Programs
    - ? Display
    - ? DirectX
    - ? Sound
    - ? The Microsoft Network
    - ? Hardware Conflict
    - ? Dial-Up Networking
    - ? Direct Cable Connection
    - ? PC Card

This troubleshooter is unable to solve your problem.

You have run into a problem that the Networking troubleshooter cannot help you solve. For more assistance, including updated troubleshooters, click **Web Help** from the **Windows Help** toolbar above, and then click **Support Online**.

< Back | Start Over

Start | ... | 5:11 PM

Step 8

If none of the suggestions offered by the troubleshooter are able to solve your problem, left click the WEB HELP button on the Windows Help toolbar and then left click Support Online.

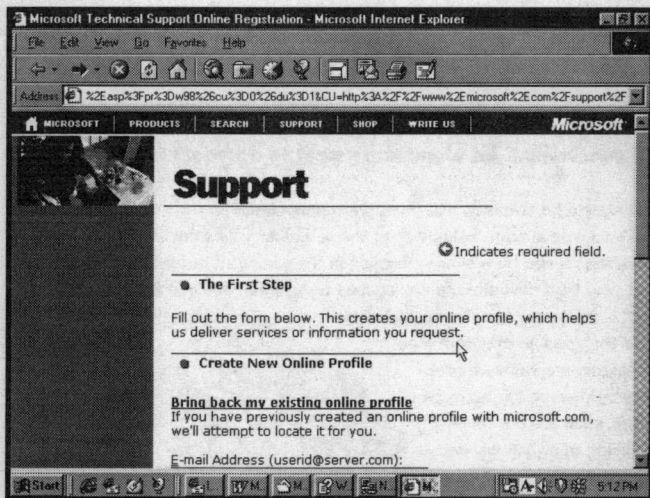

Step 9

You should then be taken directly to the Microsoft TECHNICAL SUPPORT pages. Once you have filled in the online registration form you can search for the solution to your problem.

WHAT TO DO WHEN PCS WON'T START

Computers are simple to use aren't they? Not when you run into problems just turning the PC on! Starting up a computer should be so easy, but it can suddenly become a stressful nightmare when your computer stubbornly refuses to startup, giving you some error message you can't possibly be expected to understand, let alone know what to do about it.

It should be stressed that most startup problems have a simple solution. This guide aims to help pinpoint the source of your trouble.

Solutions range from simply plugging in the computer or keyboard to finding out your hard disk storage has ceased to function. You can fix most software problems if you have the original disks and the good news is that most problems are software problems. However, hardware problems, such as your monitor refusing to switch on, do happen from time to time and, usually, you won't be able to fix the problem yourself.

If you turn your computer on and you don't see your normal messages and the friendly Windows Load screen, "Don't Panic!" This may well be easier said than done, but if there is a problem it is highly unlikely it was something that you did! It is almost impossible for you to physically damage your computer by playing with the software.

ELIMINATING HARDWARE PROBLEMS

Problem:
Your computer has a blank screen, the power or hard drive/floppy drive lights remain dark and you hear none of the familiar internal fan and hard drive noises.

Check Power
Work from the back of the computer to the power socket and check every stage in between. First push the power supply cable, making sure it's firmly home in both the computer and monitor; they can work loose. Check that the power cables work and that they have not blown a fuse. A simple way to check a power lead is to swap it with a cable you know is working. Most UK kettles use the same sort of lead. If your power lead does not work try replacing the fuse. Next, ensure that any extension leads are working and that power is flowing to your wall socket. Most modern houses have a circuit breaker trip switch - check the circuit breaker to make sure it's on. Finally, check all peripheral cables are plugged in properly.

Problem:
If the system seems to be working (the power or hard/floppy drive lights up and the fan is blowing etc.) and you still see nothing on the monitor screen, it is time to check the monitor.

Check Monitor
Check that the monitor is switched on. Most monitors are permanently left on as they take their power from the computer, so they switch on when the computer switches on. It is possible someone in you household did not know that and has turned the monitor off. Check the power indicator light is on.
If after these basic steps your computer stubbornly refuses to startup you may have a hardware problem. Before you jump on the telephone and call technical support, try reading the manuals that came with your computer. Most manuals have a troubleshooting guide, usually in the appendix at the back. These sections give solutions to commonly experienced problems there's a saying in the technical support world: "RTFM;" but being a family magazine, we couldn't possibly translate that - no prizes for guessing what it stands for though!
However, if you are still stuck, now is the time to call your help line. The tech support teams can guide you step-by-step though possible solutions as long as you tell them the symptoms.

SOFTWARE

Your computer can startup fine and you can be working away or playing a game when everything suddenly stops working. If the program you were using is causing the problem then Windows will try to give you an error message. These messages, however, are never much help to us normal people. When you see one just take it for granted that you are not going to be able to use this program until you restart your computer. Sometimes Windows will freeze altogether. You might see an hourglass that simply sits and does nothing, no matter what you do with the mouse or keyboard. In this case, you have no option but to switch off your computer and switch on again. You could loose some of your work, but this is why you should save your work often. This goes for games as well. When you switch your computer off and then restart again, Windows will tidy up any mess and, usually, your PC will now be running fine, as will the software that caused the computer to freeze in the first place (this kind of freeze is commonly known as a 'crash').

If your software is still causing problems, try uninstalling the software. It's best to do this using the Add and Remove programs feature, which you can find in the control panel. Now reinstall the software using the original discs. This should solve any data corruption problems. If all this fails, the next step is to call technical support, which could be in the form of your computer or program supplier.

As a beginner, you may be forgiven for thinking computers were put on this earth to frustrate you and make you look stupid. You may even feel like chucking the damn machine out of the window. When you get in this state - and we all have - remember that somewhere there is a answer, you are not stupid and it will invariably be a case of the solution being so simple...'once you know how.' Whether you solve your computing problems on your own or with a little help from your supplier, this troubleshooting guide should bring you closer to the solution and will certainly help you to eliminate many potential difficulties.

CRASHES AND SLOW DOWNS

If your computer passes all the above tests but still freezes during startup, try restarting your computer by switching it off then on again. Usually, Windows will startup again in the normal fashion. Sometimes, after a Windows crash, Windows's Scan disk feature will check your hard drive and clean up any errors, therefore helping your system to get going again. If this fails, you can use your Windows startup disk. Put the disk in the floppy drive before you switch on. The computer will then use the disk to start your PC. If Windows fails to load, you will be placed in DOS Mode. Now would be a good time to call your help line for a systematic guide to get you going again! Windows can be started in several ways. For instance, you can press F8 on the keyboard when you see 'Starting Windows' displayed on screen (you have to be quick or you may miss it). The simplest method would be to utilise the DOS command 'Prompt only.' From here you can tell if your hard drive and memory are OK and run several checks such, as SCANDISK and MEM. Remember, though, in this mode you really need to know a little about DOS. If you don't, find someone who does or call your help line. Windows can also run in safe mode, which is essentially a very slow, stripped down version of Windows, and which at least lets you try to find out what is wrong yourself. If you get this far, your problem will almost definitely be of the software, setup or driver variety (a driver is a small program that lets Windows control any add-on cards or peripherals that you may have connected).

TOP TIP!

You can give yourself a head start when it comes to sorting out Windows problems and diagnosing faults. Programs like Norton Utilities will auto-matically diagnose problems and fix them for you, and the great thing is that you don't need to know what is happening - all you need to know is how to run a program. Owning a copy of Norton Utilities is like having a technical support person permanently inside your computer. If you want to save yourself hours on a help line, you must buy a program like this. There are many such programs around, but Norton has been around the longest and, as such, is by far the most established (I've used Norton Utilities since 1985 - Ed.).

INKJET PRINTER TROUBLESHOOTING

With printers ranging from simple inkjets to state of the art colour lasers, you would think they would have different problems - but at the end of the day, as they essentially perform the same function, the type of errors which can occur are equally similar. Here, we take a look at inkjets...

I f you are using Windows 98 then you can use the built-in troubleshooting wizard to help you sort out your printing problems. However, to a certain extent, you can try and solve things manually. For instance, if you have sent a document to your printer and it does not appear after a reasonable amount of time, start by checking the cables connected between your printer and computer, and also look to see if the printer's power light is on; you may have forgotten to switch it on or plug it in (embarrassing, we know, but a common complaint all the same!)

Now, back to Windows. Check that the Windows printer setting has the correct printer port and printer driver selected (see the step-by-step below for more on this). If, after following the step-by-step, you still can't print your document, make sure the program from which you are printing isn't setup to send output to a file rather than the printer.

INKJET PROBLEMS

Even if you do manage to get a printout, your problems could just be beginning. If your printout is too dark or light, or if it has streaks or smears, you will need to check your printer manual to see if there is a setup program built into the printer. If so, it should be able to increase or decrease the print density, and you can sometimes do this using the printer driver. If output is too light, increase the density; if it's too dark or smears, decrease it.

If problems still persist, try using better quality paper - it really does make a difference

as cheap paper can cause smearing. If you still have smearing, you may need to replace the ink cartridge. With most makes of inkjet printer, this often solves most print quality problems. If your document prints out, but it looks splotchy, or there are parts missing, run the printer through its self-clean cycle. If that doesn't work, then replacing the ink cartridge is probably the best bet.

If your document prints, but it looks like pages of gobbledegook, re-check the printer configuration in your software. All printers use one of several printer languages to tell it how to print a page. If you have the wrong printer drive selected, it's possible to send a Postscript printer language document to your inkjet printer, and all you'll get is rubbish.

TOP TIP!

This tip was sent in by one of our readers and could save you lots of money!

"I thought your many readers might be interested in the following very BIG money saving tip. My inkjet printer recently developed a fault, namely no black printing, even after numerous cleans and replacement of the cartridge/s. As I work in the computer maintenance field, I have a number of experienced people to call on. The diagnosis of the problem was as follows:

As this was one of two printers that I have on line, the other one being a mono laser and the most frequently used, the inkjet and lain idle for nearly a month over the Christmas/New Year period, and the ink had dried in the printer head. This is a known problem concerning inkjets within the trade, caused by under-used printers placed in a central heated environment. The solution? Replace the very costly print head and ink cartridges, clean the machine and restart. And the cost? Nearly as much as the printer would cost to replace as new! However, a very good preventative measure, if the printer is likely to lay idle for some time, would be to run a nozzle check and print test pages at least once a week.

What I did do, as it was too late for the 'preventative measure', was replace my printer, with an new one, costing £165. So, in the end, a very costly lesson, and one that is not pointed out in the manufacturer's manuals! Hope your readers take note."
Mrs Joan D Lee

INKJET TROUBLE SHOOTING

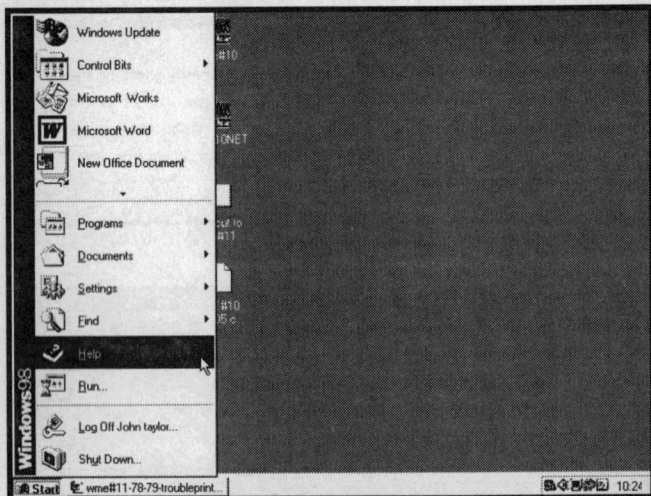

Step 1

You will find the PRINT trouble shooter in the Windows HELP system, which can be found with a left click on the Start button menu.

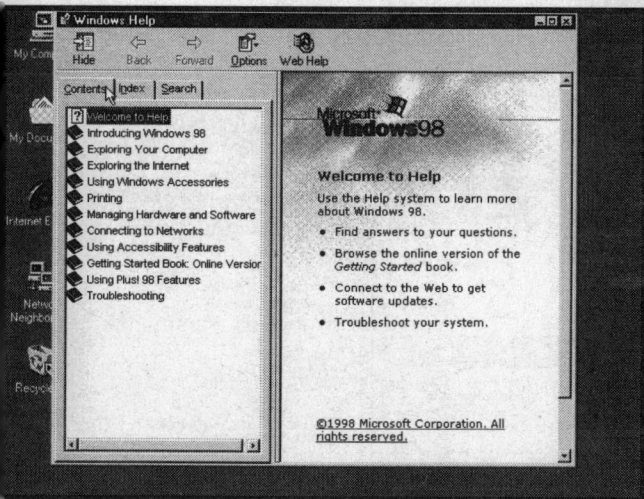

Step 2

First, locate the CONTENTS tab and click the left mouse button. A list of the different help items will be listed.

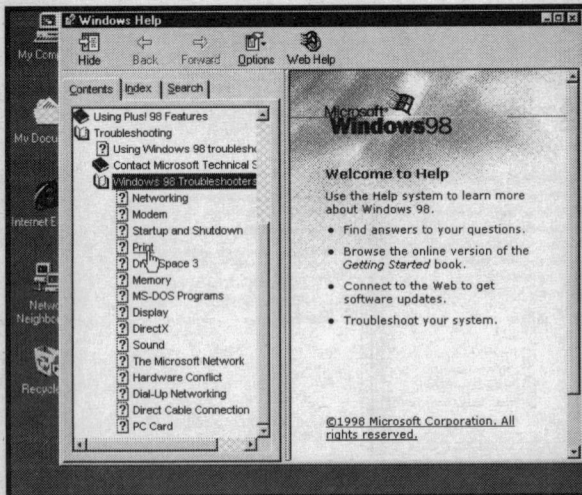

Step 3

Next, move the mouse pointer to TROUBLESHOOTING and left click. Then, select 'Windows 98 Troubleshooters' and, finally, choose the Print wizard.

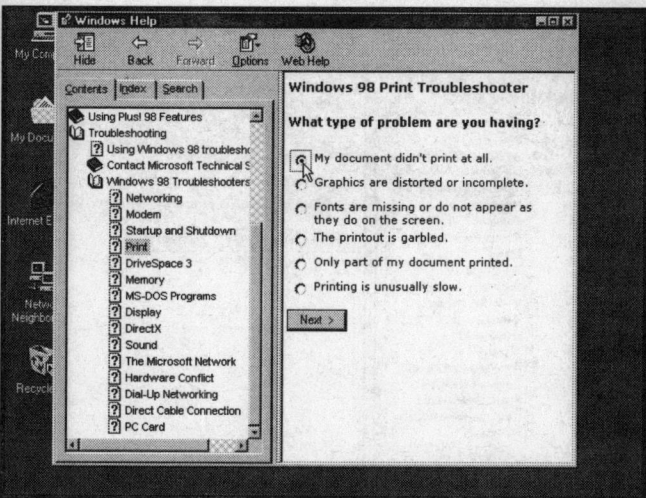

Windows Help

Hide | Back | Forward | Options | Web Help

Contents | Index | Search

- Using Plus! 98 Features
- Troubleshooting
  - [?] Using Windows 98 troublesho
  - Contact Microsoft Technical S
  - Windows 98 Troubleshooters
    - [?] Networking
    - [?] Modem
    - [?] Startup and Shutdown
    - [?] Print
    - [?] DriveSpace 3
    - [?] Memory
    - [?] MS-DOS Programs
    - [?] Display
    - [?] DirectX
    - [?] Sound
    - [?] The Microsoft Network
    - [?] Hardware Conflict
    - [?] Dial-Up Networking
    - [?] Direct Cable Connection
    - [?] PC Card

Windows 98 Print Troubleshooter

What type of problem are you having?

- My document didn't print at all.
- Graphics are distorted or incomplete.
- Fonts are missing or do not appear as they do on the screen.
- The printout is garbled.
- Only part of my document printed.
- Printing is unusually slow.

Next >

Step 4

You will now be presented with a list of QUESTIONS. Move the mouse pointer to the circle next to the question that matches your problem and left click the mouse - the circle will be filled with a black dot.

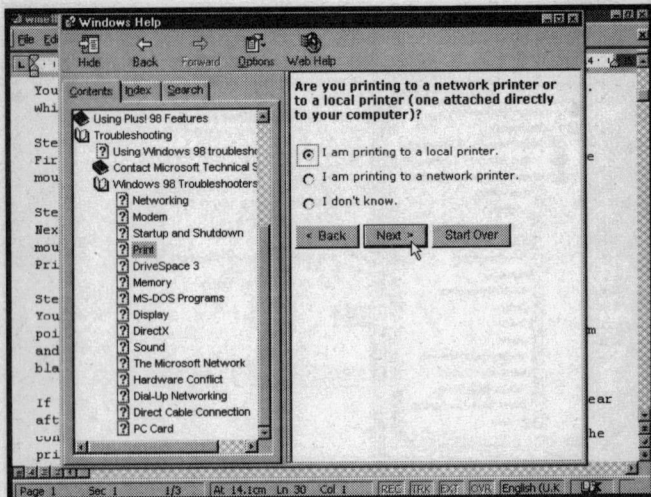

Windows Help

File Ed...

Hide Back Forward Options Web Help

Contents | Index | Search

Using Plus! 98 Features
Troubleshooting
  ? Using Windows 98 troublesh...
  ? Contact Microsoft Technical S...
  Windows 98 Troubleshooters
  ? Networking
  ? Modem
  ? Startup and Shutdown
  ? Print
  ? DriveSpace 3
  ? Memory
  ? MS-DOS Programs
  ? Display
  ? DirectX
  ? Sound
  ? The Microsoft Network
  ? Hardware Conflict
  ? Dial-Up Networking
  ? Direct Cable Connection
  ? PC Card

Are you printing to a network printer or to a local printer (one attached directly to your computer)?

- I am printing to a local printer.
- I am printing to a network printer.
- I don't know.

‹ Back   Next ›   Start Over

Page 1   Sec 1   1/3   At 14.1cm   Ln 30   Col 1   REC TRK EXT OVR   English (U.K

Step 5

Now go to the button marked Next and left click. You will be asked another QUESTION; repeat step four to select your answer.

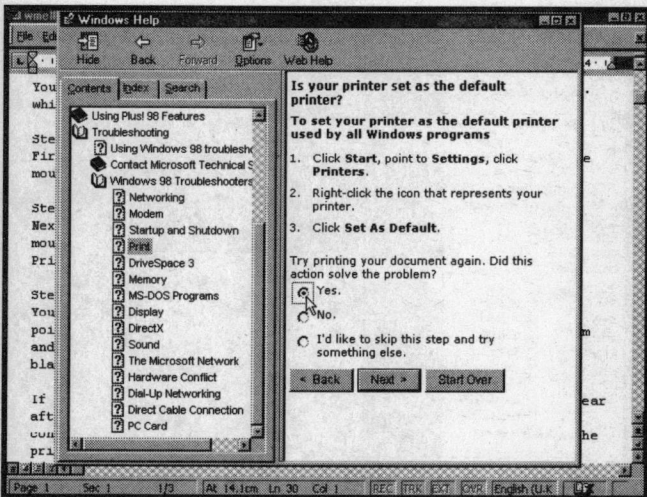

Windows Help

File Ed...

Hide Back Forward Options Web Help

Contents | Index | Search |

Using Plus! 98 Features
Troubleshooting
  ? Using Windows 98 troublesho
  ● Contact Microsoft Technical S
  Windows 98 Troubleshooters
    ? Networking
    ? Modem
    ? Startup and Shutdown
    ? Print
    ? DriveSpace 3
    ? Memory
    ? MS-DOS Programs
    ? Display
    ? DirectX
    ? Sound
    ? The Microsoft Network
    ? Hardware Conflict
    ? Dial-Up Networking
    ? Direct Cable Connection
    ? PC Card

Is your printer set as the default printer?

To set your printer as the default printer used by all Windows programs

1. Click **Start**, point to **Settings**, click **Printers**.

2. Right-click the icon that represents your printer.

3. Click **Set As Default**.

Try printing your document again. Did this action solve the problem?

○ Yes.
○ No.

○ I'd like to skip this step and try something else.

< Back   Next >   Start Over

Page 1   Sec 1   1/3   At 14.1cm Ln 30 Col 1   REC TRK EXT OVR English (U.K

Step 6

Left click the Next button again. You will be given a step-by-step SOLUTION. If the suggested solution does not work, don't worry - you can easily try other ones.

CHECKING YOUR PRINTER SETTINGS

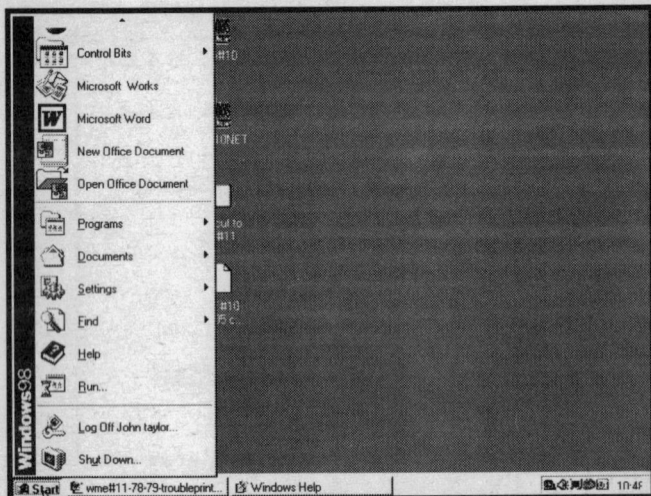

Control Bits	▶
Microsoft Works	
Microsoft Word	
New Office Document	
Open Office Document	
Programs	▶
Documents	▶
Settings	▶
Find	▶
Help	
Run...	
Log Off John taylor...	
Shut Down...	

Windows98

🏁 Start | wme#11-78-79-troubleprint... | 📖 Windows Help | | 10:4F

Step 1
To find the settings, move the mouse pointer to the START BUTTON and left click the mouse.

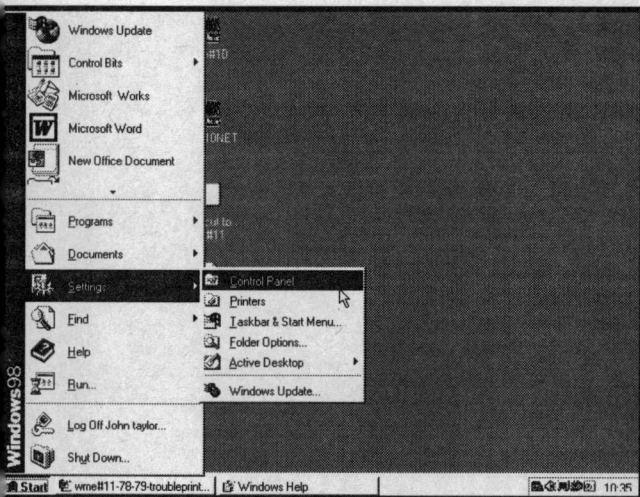

Windows Update		
Control Bits ▸		#10
Microsoft Works		
Microsoft Word		|ONET
New Office Document		
Programs ▸		ut to
Documents ▸		#11
Settings ▸	Control Panel	
Find ▸	Printers	
Help	Taskbar & Start Menu...	
Run...	Folder Options...	
Log Off John taylor...	Active Desktop ▸	
Shut Down...	Windows Update...	

Start | wme#11-78-79-troubleprint... | Windows Help | 10:35

Step 2
Move the mouse pointer to SETTINGS and then across to PRINTERS.
Select this with a left click. This will open a folder onscreen.

033

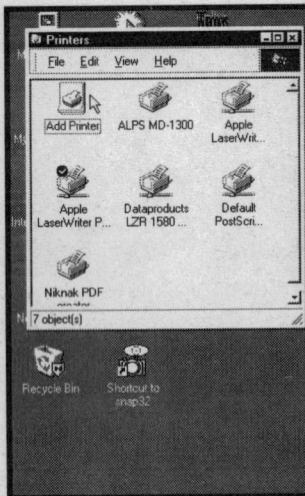

Step 3

If no printer can be found in this folder, double left click on 'Add a NEW PRINTER' and follow the wizard's onscreen instructions.

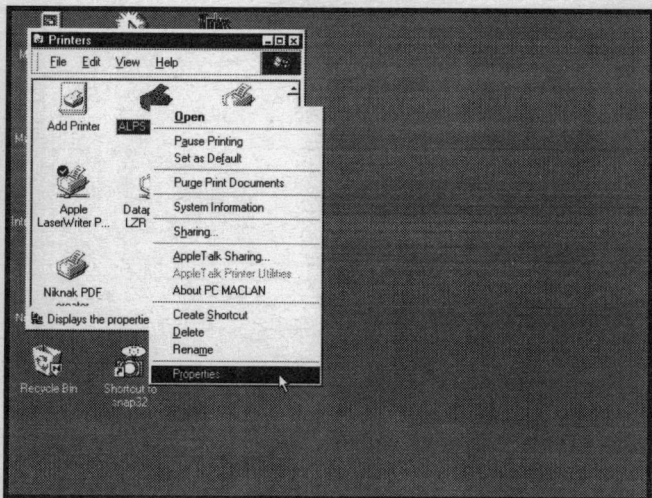

Step 4

If your printer is there, right click the mouse on the printers icon and, when the list pops up, select PROPERTIES and left click.

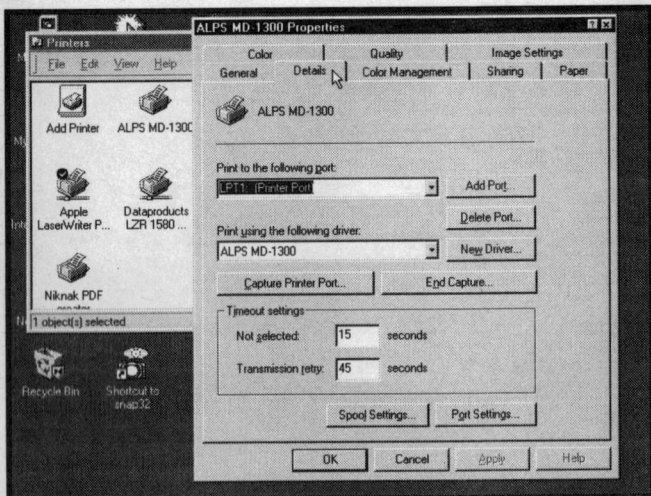

ALPS MD-1300 Properties

| Color | | Quality | | Image Settings |
| General | Details | Color Management | Sharing | Paper |

ALPS MD-1300

Print to the following port:
LPT1: (Printer Port)   [Add Port...]
                        [Delete Port...]

Print using the following driver:
ALPS MD-1300   [New Driver...]

[Capture Printer Port...] [End Capture...]

Timeout settings
Not selected: 15   seconds
Transmission retry: 45   seconds

[Spool Settings...] [Port Settings...]

[OK] [Cancel] [Apply] [Help]

Step 5

Now move the mouse pointer to the tab called DETAILS and check the setting you find there to make sure your printer is properly set up.

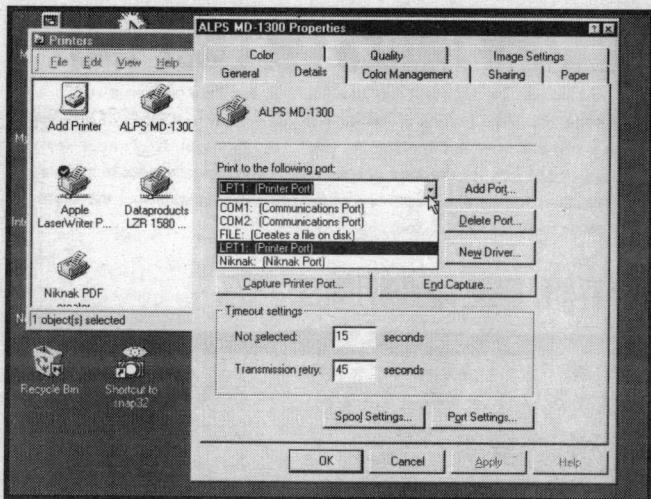

Step 6

To change the PRINTER PORT, move the mouse pointer to the down arrow at the side of the box marked 'Print to the following port' and left click. Now select your printer port from the drop-down list.

LOOK FOR THE OBVIOUS...

These steps may seem obvious, but you may be surprised how easy they are to forget.

- Make sure the printer is switched on.
- Make sure the power and printer cables are securely plugged in.
- If the printer is plugged into an extension lead, make sure it is on as well.
- Check the actual printer for any error messages on LCD displays or error lights.
- Make sure the printer is ready to print; a light saying ready or online should be lit.
- Check to see that the printer has paper.
- Make sure there is no paper jammed inside the printer.

CREATING TABLES THE EASY WAY

Many people are frightened of using tables, but they provide a very straightforward means of setting out lots of different kinds of information in a tidy and readable fashion. As you'll see, the neat thing about them is that they're not just for the kind of information you would expect in a table. They are great for rows and columns of figures and statistics, but there are many other uses for tables, too.

STEP BY STEP GUIDE: CREATING TABLES

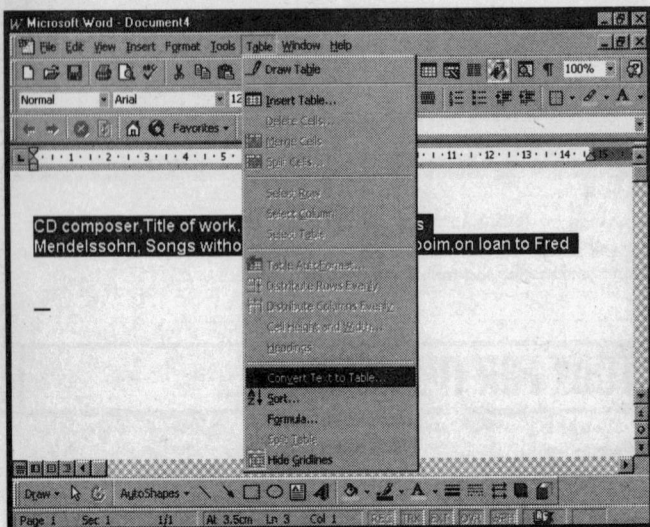

STEP 1
Type in something like this in your document, as two lines with items separated by commas:

CD composer,Title of work,Performer(s),Where it is

Mendelssohn, Songs without words,Daniel Barenboim,on loan to Fred

Then, highlight them and opt for Table, Convert Text to Table.

Convert Text to Table

Number of columns: [ ] OK

Number of rows: [ ] Cancel

Column width: Auto AutoFormat...

Table format: (none)

Separate text at:
- ○ Paragraphs ○ Commas
- ○ Tabs ● Other: [ ]

CD composer,Title of w...

Mendelssohn, Songs w... Fred

CD composer	Title of work	Performer(s)	Where it is
Mendelssohn	Songs without words	Daniel Barenboim	on loan to Fred

STEP 2

When the dialog box appears, just click on OK. Lo and behold, you have created your first table. Or rather, Word has done all the hard work for you. The composite image shows the dialog box and the resulting table.

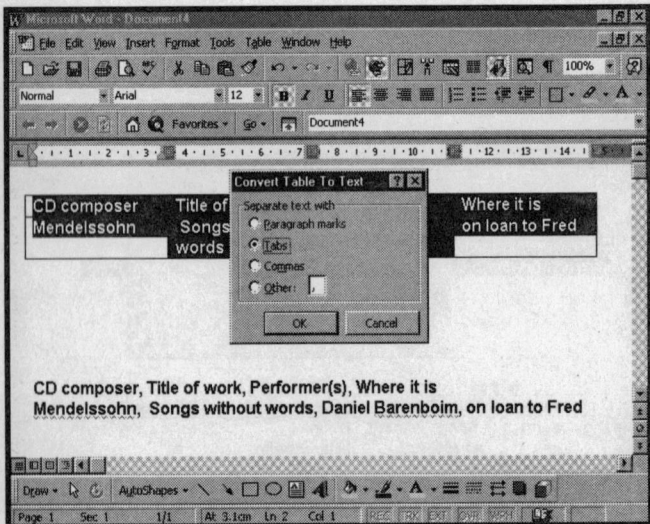

Microsoft Word - Document4

File Edit View Insert Format Tools Table Window Help

Normal ▾ Arial ▾ 12 ▾ **B** *I* U

Favorites ▾ Go ▾ Document4

Convert Table To Text

Separate text with
- ○ Paragraph marks
- ● Tabs
- ○ Commas
- ○ Other:

OK   Cancel

CD composer	Title of		Where it is
Mendelssohn	Songs		on loan to Fred
	words		

CD composer, Title of work, Performer(s), Where it is
Mendelssohn, Songs without words, Daniel Barenboim, on loan to Fred

Draw ▾ AutoShapes ▾

Page 1   Sec 1   1/1   At 3.1cm   Ln 2   Col 1

STEP 3

Now highlight everything inside the table. Click on Table, Convert Table to Text and, when the dialog box appears, either accept tabs as separators or opt for commas again, and there is your table automatically back as plain text. The image shows the two stages in the operation.

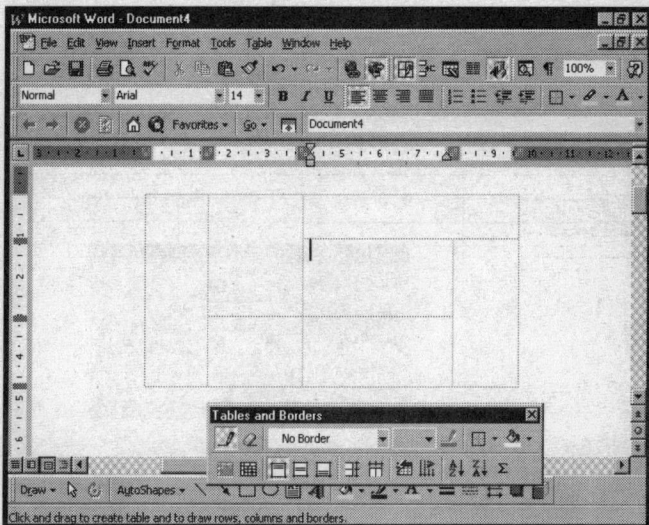

Microsoft Word - Document4

File Edit View Insert Format Tools Table Window Help

Normal | Arial | 14 | B I U | Favorites ▾ Go ▾ | Document4

Tables and Borders
No Border

Draw ▾ AutoShapes ▾

Click and drag to create table and to draw rows, columns and borders.

STEP 4

That's the simplest approach – but you can create tables in other ways, too.
Go to Table, Draw Table and use the pencil shaped cursor to draw a box outline first, then the individual rows and columns. The lines will automatically
appear vertically and horizontally; there's no need to draw the full line. You
don't have to create a uniform grid, either – you can create the most diverse
pattern to suit your needs

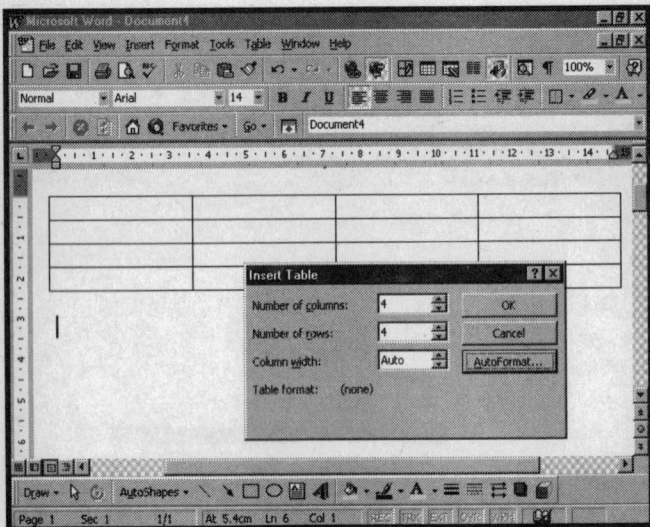

STEP 5

Alternatively, go to Insert Table, specifying the number of rows and columns you want. This is the easiest approach if you want a fairly simple table, but the edit facilities are good enough to allow you to do just about anything with a table that's already been created, so it's up to you to choose the option which suits you best.

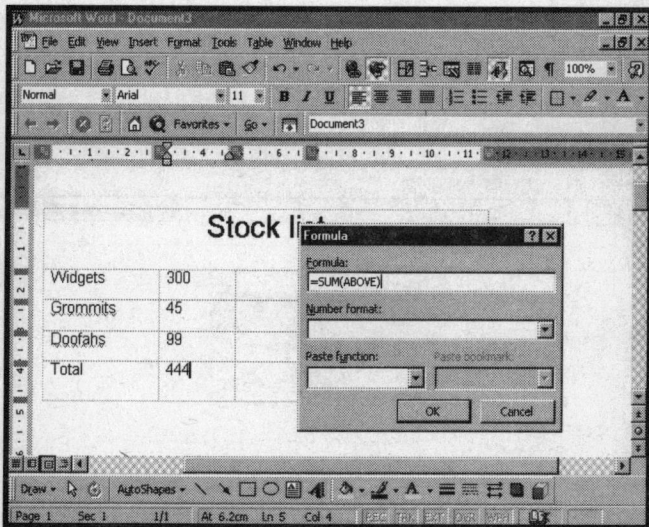

STEP 6

You can even put formulae into cells as you would in a simple spreadsheet.
Here I am adding up a column, and the Formula dialog box is even second-
guessing for me what the formula is that I'm after.

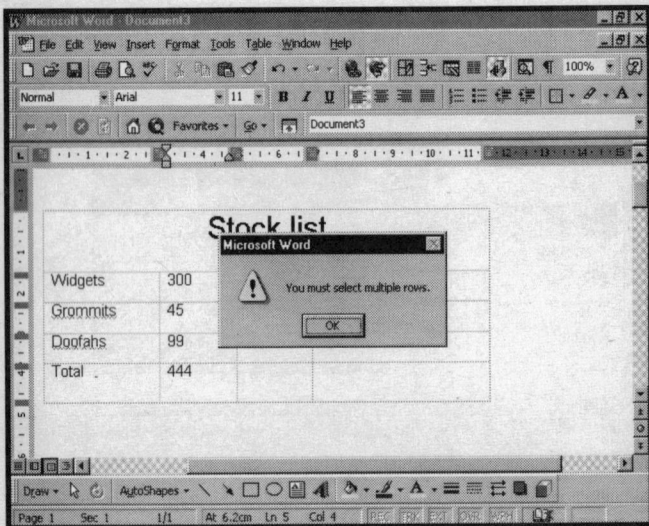

STEP 7

If you have created your table freehand, you can even up the rows and columns if you wish, but as the error message shows, you must select an appropriate area first. You can also vary height and width by holding the cursor over a line until it changes into the line-moving pointer – then drag the line back and forth as you wish.

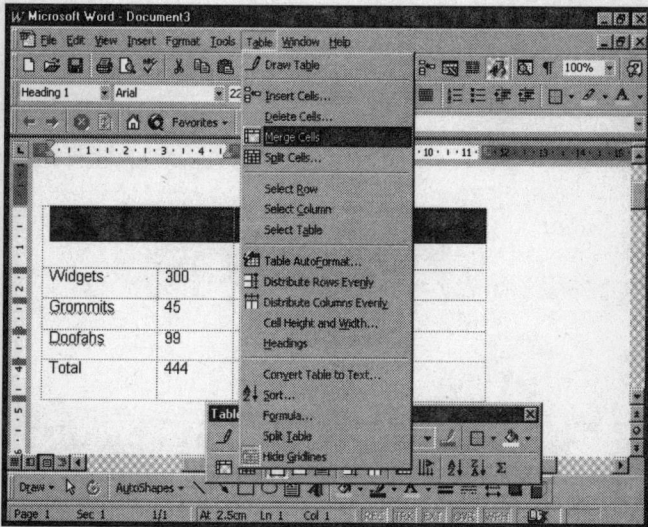

STEP 8

To create a heading, or to employ other similar effects, you can merge cells by highlighting them and selecting Merge cells from the Table menu.

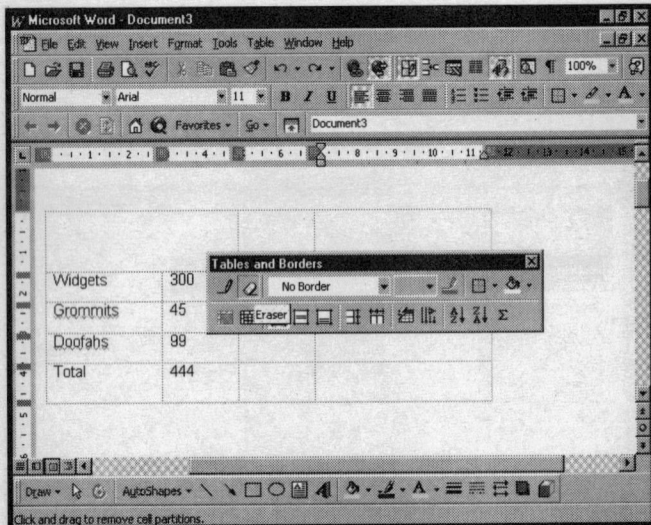

STEP 9

You can also split cells and use the eraser on the Tables and Borders toolbar to remove lines. The eraser tool is just to the right of the line drawing tool.

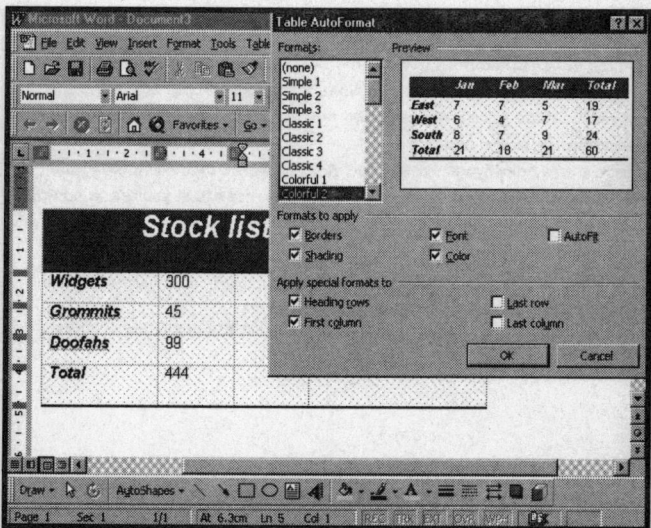

STEP 10

Try autoformatting a table to achieve a particular effect. You can also hide
the gridlines – so nobody realises that it is a table at all. This works well
for book lists, for example, or for special layout effects on the printed
page or screen.

JUMPING ABOUT

One of the key features of Windows 98 is that it is aiming towards a situation where you don't actually know – or care – where your document is. It can be sitting on your local machine or on a computer half way round the world.

As such, you can create so-called links (or hyperlinks) in your document, pointing either to different parts of the same document, to other documents of yours, to pages on your local network (if you are on one) or the Internet. All this can be done relatively easily, and enables people to hop back and forth to different parts of the text.

In fact, that's how 'hypertext' got its name. It means text which isn't read sequentially, like a novel from beginning to end, but which you are in control of, in the sense that where there is a link you can choose to jump to it or not, as the case may be.

This is how it's done.
(Note: Let's assume you have a list of contents at the beginning of a document, called Section one, Section two, and so on.)

STEP BY STEP GUIDE: HYPERLINKS

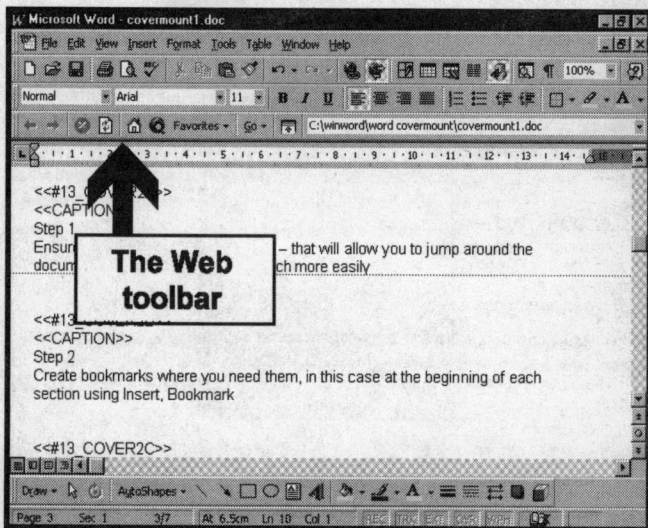

STEP 1
The first step is to ensure that the Web toolbar is visible – that will allow you to jump around the document or between documents much more easily

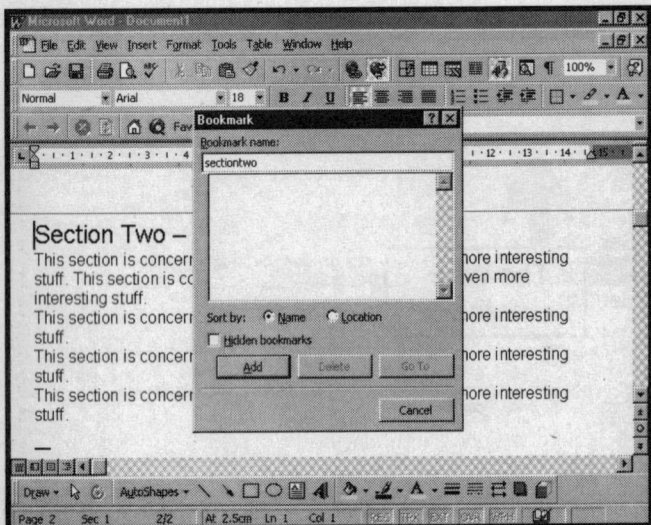

STEP 2

Create bookmarks where you need them - in this case, at the beginning of each section - using Insert, Bookmark

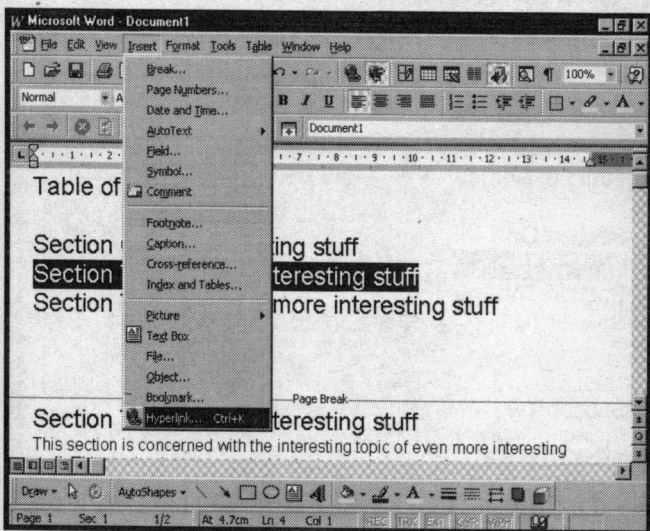

Microsoft Word - Document1

File Edit View Insert Format Tools Table Window Help

Insert menu:
- Break...
- Page Numbers...
- Date and Time...
- AutoText
- Field...
- Symbol...
- Comment
- Footnote...
- Caption...
- Cross-reference...
- Index and Tables...
- Picture
- Text Box
- File...
- Object...
- Bookmark...
- Hyperlink... Ctrl+K

Normal

Table of

Section ...ing stuff
Section ...teresting stuff
Section ...more interesting stuff

————Page Break————

Section ...teresting stuff
This section is concerned with the interesting topic of even more interesting

Draw AutoShapes

Page 1   Sec 1   1/2   At 4.7cm Ln 4 Col 1

STEP 3

Establish your list of contents using the Hyperlink option on the Insert menu
by first selecting the text you want to use as a link, opting for Insert, then
Hyperlink (or use the keyboard shortcut, Ctrl+K).

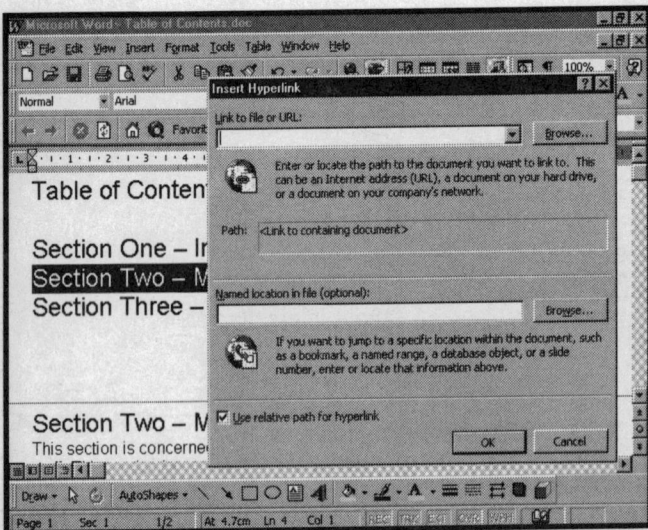

STEP 4

Up pops the Hyperlink dialog box. At this point, you should first have saved the current document, otherwise you will get an error message – the system needs to know where the file is going to be before a link can be set up.

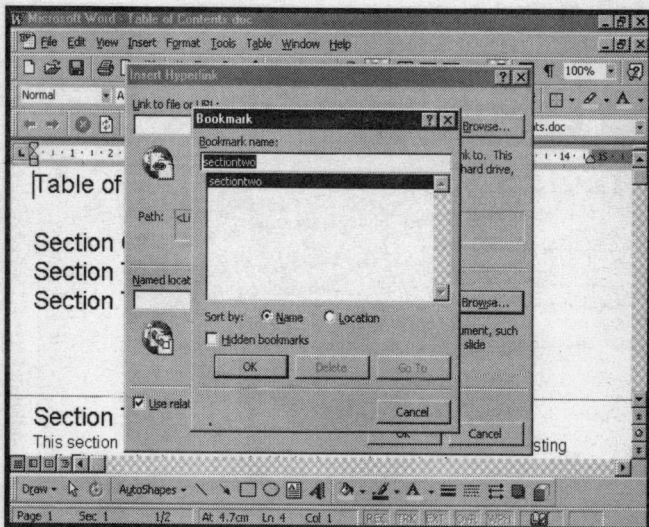

STEP 5

What you do now depends on where you want to jump to. If it's in the same document, go to the location in the file edit box and put in the name of the Bookmark.

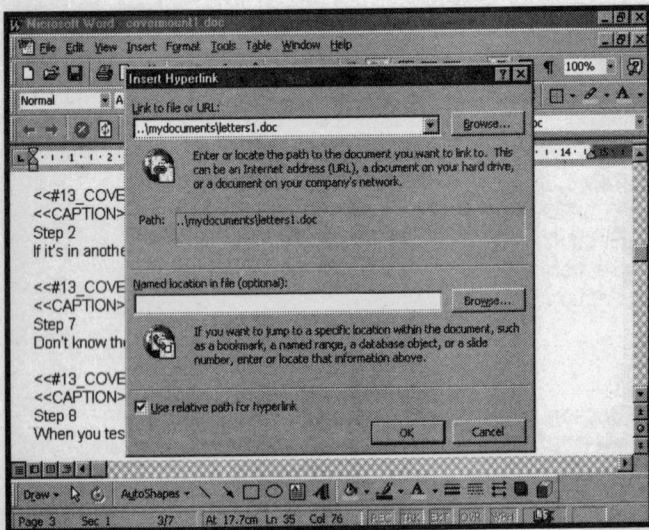

STEP 6

Alternately, if it's in another file, enter the path in the first edit box, as shown here.

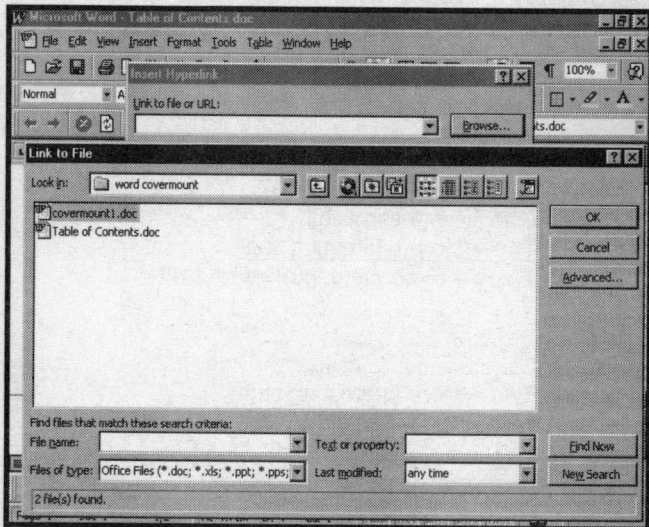

STEP 7

Don't know the path or unhappy about typing it? Use the Browse button instead.

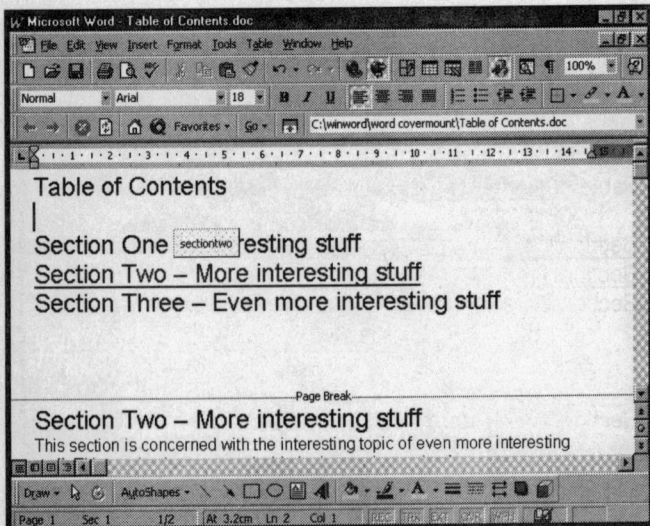

STEP 8

When you test the link out, you will see the address in a little hint box. You may have to change the size of the underlined text to match your requirements.

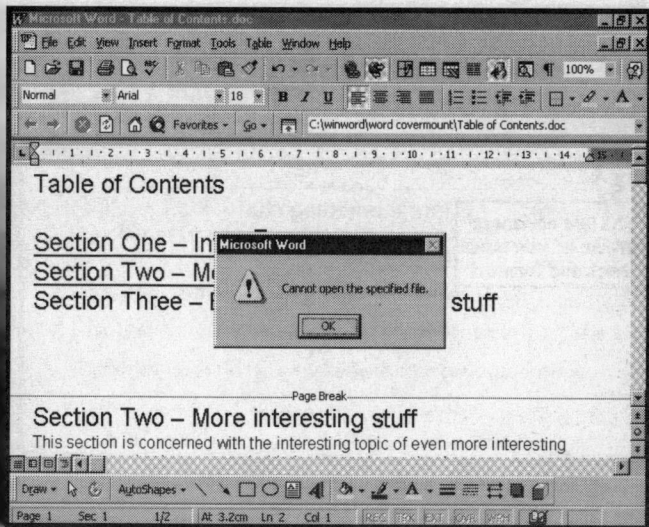

STEP 9

If you get the bookmark name wrong within the current file, you jump to the beginning of the file – but if you misname a file or address elsewhere, you get this error message.

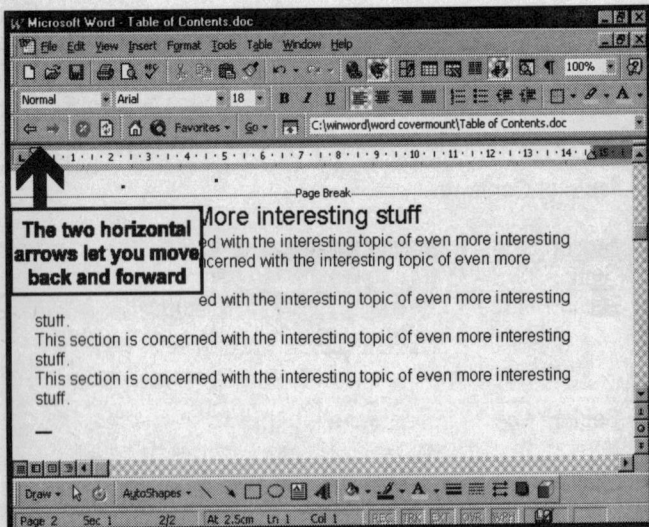

The two horizontal arrows let you move back and forward

STEP 10

Use the Web toolbar to aid your navigation. Hold the mouse pointer over the other icons to see what they mean.

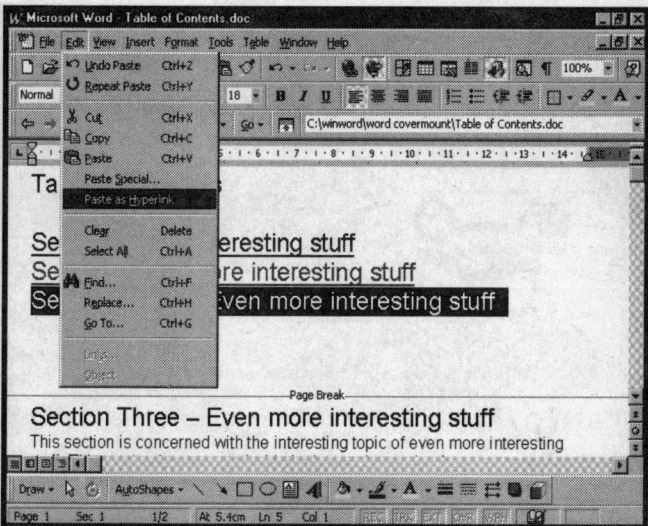

STEP 11

Another way to jump within a piece of text is to highlight the text you want to jump to, copy it to the clipboard, then move to where you want the jump to end up. Then use the Edit menu to 'Paste as Hyperlink.' That makes sense when, for example, you want to jump to somewhere in the text and you are happy to use the text at that point as the name for the link.

STEP 12

There's nothing to stop you using an image as a link. Highlight the image, go for Insert, Hyperlink and then carry on as in step two.

TEN HYPERLINK HINTS AND TIPS

1. You can jump to Excel, Access, PowerPoint, Outlook Express documents - and you can create Hyperlinks in the same way as you would in Word.

2. In Excel, you can jump to a previously named range. Select the range, then click on the Name drop-down box in the top left-hand corner of the screen and finally name the link.

3. Note that links go blue and, once they have been clicked on, they turn magenta. When the document is reloaded, links are all reset to blue.

4. If you want to edit a Hyperlink for any reason, place the mouse pointer over it until it turns into the hand shape, then right click on it. On the pop-up menu move down to Hyperlink, then go for Edit Hyperlink. Up comes the Edit Hyperlink dialog box.

5. On the Hyperlink dialog box, 'relative names' means that you name the target file in relation to where your current file is. 'Absolute addresses' mean the full path or name, and you would tend to use that option less often.

6. Avoid punctuation marks in links as they can cause difficulties, especially the hash sign.

7. If you don't highlight text first, then select Insert Hyperlink. The address of your target file appears as the link, together with the location within the file…as long as you have specified it first.

8. If you type something which Word recognises as an email or Internet address, Word will underline it for you if you have the right settings in Autoformat. Go to Format, Autoformat, Options, 'Autoformat as you type.' Check the box which offers to underline 'Internet and network paths with hyperlinks.'

9. If you have the option 'Convert to Hyperlink' switched on and you want a particular link not to be underlined (in other words, to appear as plain text), use the arrow keys (not the mouse) to move the insert pointer over the link. Then press Crtl+Shift+F9 and the link will lose its underline and become plain text.

10. Certain characters are not allowed in bookmarks, including spaces. To find out if a character is legal, type it in and, if the result isn't a valid book-mark, all the options except Cancel go grey and you can't access them.

USING LINKS FOR TEACHING

One great application for links in and between documents is in teaching. For example, you could put a poem up on screen and link particular words and phrases to notes you have written, or you could set up a piece of foreign text or text for translation, and add notes and help wherever you want it.

...Or you could create a multiple choice test, where one answer can be marked as correct, the rest as wrong.

TEMPLATES FOR ALL

Nothing could be simpler than setting up a template to make your work more productive – and save you time and effort. A template is nothing more frightening than a blank document with various bits and pieces filled in for you already to save you the trouble of doing so.

The simplest one of all for you to try is headed notepaper. Open a blank document, then create your own headed paper.

This composite shows your letterhead and the drop-down menu from which you select a template file which will by default be saved in the Templates folder.

Don't save it as a DOC file, though, go to the drop-down list and opt for a DOT file. This will save your efforts as a template in the General section of the templates.

In general, for your own personal and small business use, it can be a far better option to have your headed paper stored electronically, because (a) it saves having to buy in printed paper in bulk, because the moment you do so the phone number changes, or you get a new member of staff or something else happens; and (b), it's far more flexible, as you can customise the headed paper depending on who is sending out the letter, and you can easily have A4, A5, memo format, compliments slips and the rest all ready to hand.

If you really must buy in some fancy headed paper on embossed paper in glorious colour, do consider putting the minimum information on the pre-printed paper and adding customised details yourself at the top of each letter. This can be done with a series of templates.

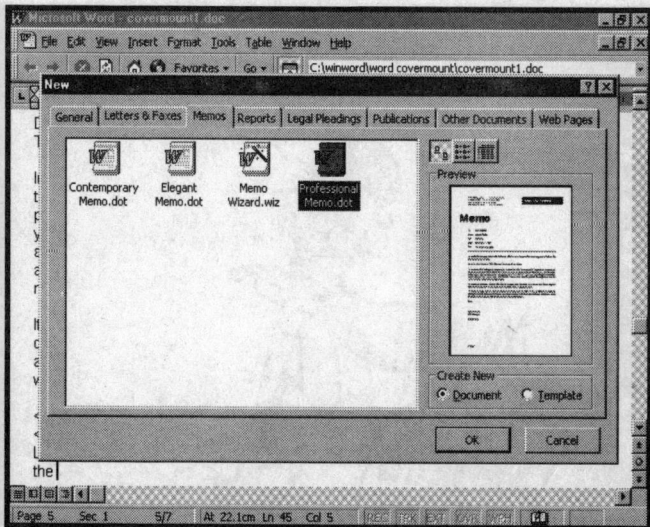

Look at the templates which Word already has on offer for you. This is the memo selection, with the Professional memo template being previewed.

BROWSING THROUGH YOUR DOCUMENTS

Why not learn to use the Document Browser to help you find your way quickly round your documents? It's situated at the bottom right-hand corner of the window, just below the vertical scrollbar. Find the button with the circle in the middle, the Select Browse Object button. Click on that and a tool-bar appears with no less than ten options on it. From left to right, top row first, they are:

Go To
Edit
Find
Heading
Graphic
Table
Field
Endnote
Footnote
Comment
Section
Page

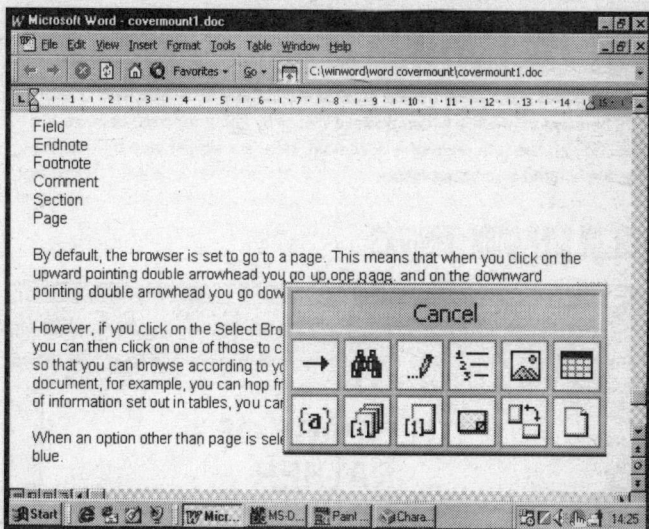

W Microsoft Word - covermount1.doc

File Edit View Insert Format Tools Table Window Help

C:\winword\word covermount\covermount1.doc

Field
Endnote
Footnote
Comment
Section
Page

By default, the browser is set to go to a page. This means that when you click on the upward pointing double arrowhead you go up one page, and on the downward pointing double arrowhead you go dow

Cancel

However, if you click on the Select Bro
you can then click on one of those to c
so that you can browse according to yo
document, for example, you can hop fr
of information set out in tables, you car

When an option other than page is sele
blue.

Start | Micr... | MS-D... | Paint... | Chara... | 14:25

An enlarged image of the basic ten options which you can select.

By default, the browser is set to go to a page. This means that when you click on the upward pointing double-arrowhead you go up one page, and on the downward pointing double-arrowhead you go down one page.

However, if you click on the Select Browse Object button and the ten options appear, you can then click on one of those to change the function of the double-arrowheads. This means that you can browse according to your selected criterion. If you have a large document, for example, you can hop from one section to another, or if you have a lot of information set out in tables, you can jump from one table to another.

When an option other than page is selected, the double-headed arrows change to blue. If you want to browse for other items, click on the Go To option and then make your choice from the dialog box.

OUT ON THE BORDER

Sometimes a document could do with brightening up a little, and one of the ways in which you can achieve this is by going for page borders, especially on the title page of a document. Here's a simple step-by-step way to achieve quite a startling result:

STEP BY STEP GUIDE: BORDERS

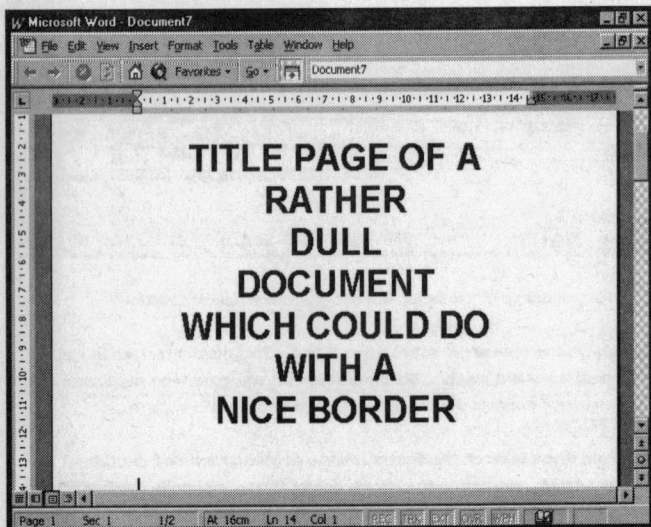

STEP 1

Start off with your rather dull title page and ensure that it is all ready for embellishment.

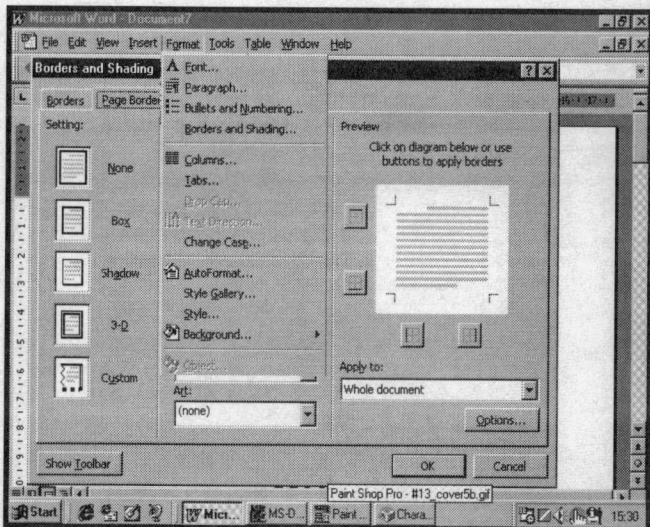

STEP 2

This composite shows the Format menu and the Page border tab of the Borders and Shading dialog box. If you don't want to affect your whole document, ensure that you opt to 'Border this page only.'

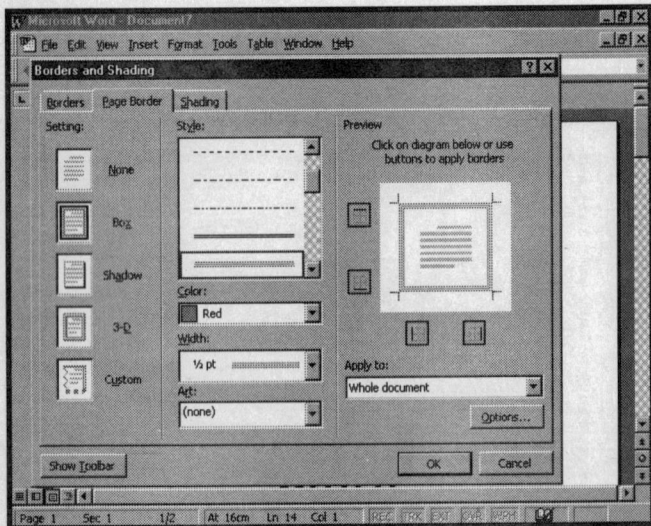

STEP 3

You could brighten things up with this simple outline – and put it in colour, as previewed for you on the right-hand side of the screen

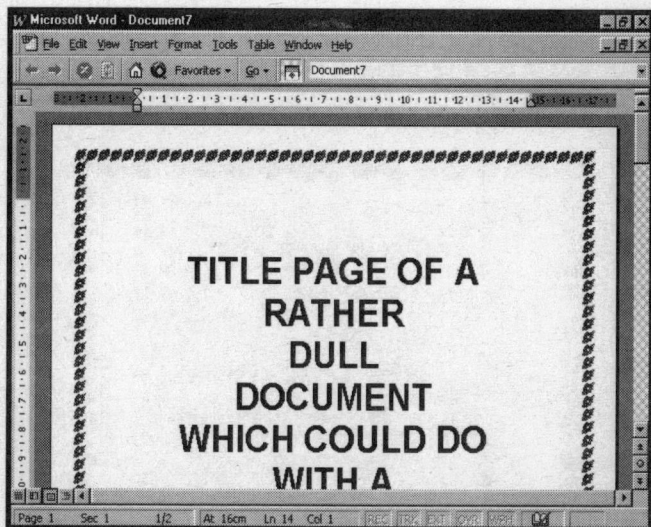

Microsoft Word - Document7

File Edit View Insert Format Tools Table Window Help

Favorites ▾ Go ▾ Document7

TITLE PAGE OF A
RATHER
DULL
DOCUMENT
WHICH COULD DO
WITH A

Page 1   Sec 1   1/2   At 16cm   Ln 14   Col 1

STEP 4

But why not be adventurous? Click on the Art drop-down menu and select one
of the wide choice of options. To remove the border, go to the Page border
tab and select None as the page border.

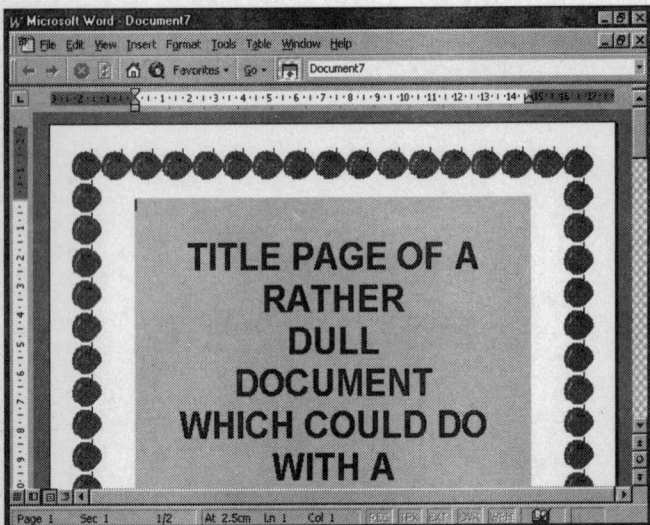

W Microsoft Word - Document7

File Edit View Insert Format Tools Table Window Help

← → ⊗ ⟳ ⌂ ✿ Favorites ▾ Go ▾ 📄 Document7

TITLE PAGE OF A
RATHER
DULL
DOCUMENT
WHICH COULD DO
WITH A

Page 1   Sec 1   1/2   At 2.5cm Ln 1   Col 1

STEP 5

Alternatively, you could go one better by selecting Shading, highlighting the text, and going for a nice colour background as well as a cheerful border. Then everyone will want to read your boring document.

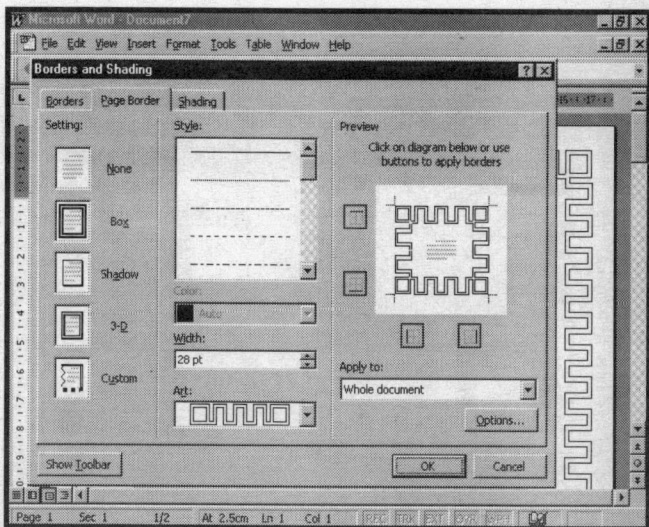

STEP 6

To vary the size of the border or border art, change the value in the Width box. Here, it is set to 28 point.

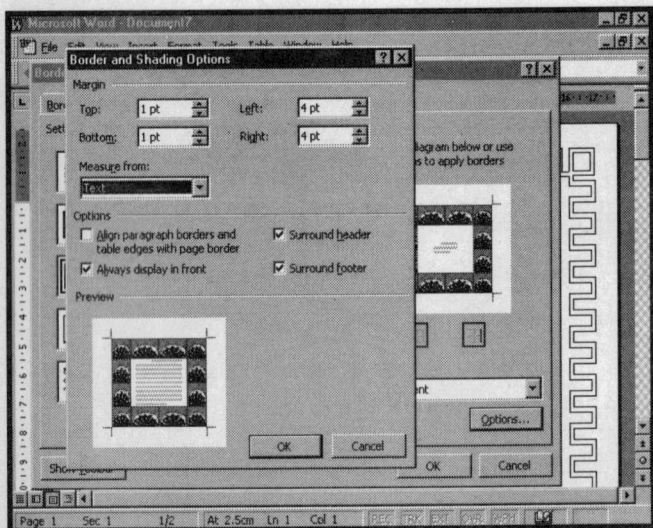

STEP 7

For advanced choices, click on the Options tab, then change the Measure to 'from text.' That will allow you to surround Headers and Footers. This will also allow you to overcome any problems you might have if your border goes beyond the printable area of your printer. A little trial and error will ensure that your border appears as it should.

QUESTIONS AND ANSWERS

IN A MODEM MUDDLE

Q The SupraExpress 336i, which came with my PC, works perfectly (and quietly). My answering machine is part of the local Telecom service, and sometimes incoming calls cut my `net connection. Unless the room is very quiet, you don't hear the modem dropping out and double-clicking the "connect"" icon shows that I am still connected. I downloaded a small application, called Dunce - but, like the computer, it also doesn't recognise the drop-out and so is wasted, and when the modem drops out at the very last moment, with literally one second and one percent left to download, it is extremely annoying to say the least. Your thoughts, virtual or real, would be very much appreciated.

A This problem has cropped up a few times before, and we have been in touch with both Supra and British Telecom regarding this unusual (but highly annoying) problem. Although neither side would admit it was their fault directly, it was generally decided that it is the answering service that is at fault. Get in contact with the BT support line and see if they can sort it out - it is very unlikely to be the modem!

JUNGLE MUSIC

Q I left a friend of mine (at least, I thought he was a friend) to play some game or other on my machine, and when he left there was a rather mysterious smirk on his face. I put that down to his having achieved genius status at noughts and crosses, but I soon discovered that he had somehow messed around with the sounds on my computer.

Instead of the normal bells and raspberries, I heard all these strange animalistic grunts and groans, some of them hinting at an animal in a deal of pain or in urgent need of the toilet. What on earth has he done and how can I reverse the damage?

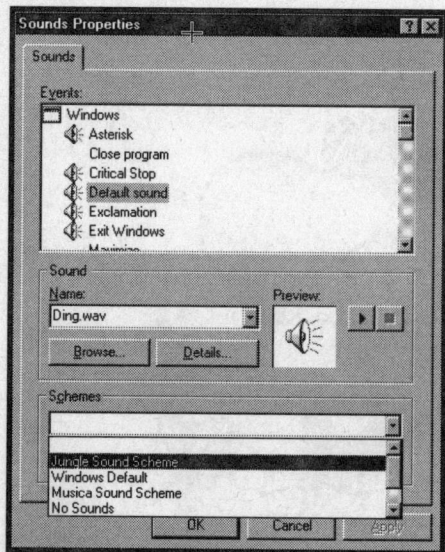

A Trade him in for another friend. Then go to the Control Panel, double click on Sounds and up will come Sounds Properties. Our guess is that you will find a reference to jungle sounds under Schemes. You can change that back to Windows default, replace it with your own scheme, or turn the wretched things off altogether.

RGB & HSL EXPLAINED

Q What's the difference between RGB and HSL and what difference does it make?

A RGB stands for Red, green and blue, and values for each vary between 0-255. With all values at zero you get black; with all at 255, you have white. All the other colours are represented by values in between. Hue, saturation and luminance - which is what HSL stands for - is essentially a different way of expressing the same values.

OUT OF CONTROL

Q OK, so it's nice when Windows 95 changes your clock for you to Daylight Saving Time. But I think it's a bit over the top when Word 97 insists on overruling you by putting the "th" in 30th as a superscript, and also forces the format of numbered paragraphs. Don't you just love it when you're not in control?

A Too true. We must confess that we actually preferred the bad old days of MS-DOS, when you were at least in control of what was going on and there was no one else to blame if the system blew up in your face. Now there is so much happening behind the scenes which you aren't aware of and which few of us have the knowledge to patch up when it all goes horribly pear-shaped.

The answer to your problem is buried away in the Tools menu. Click on the AutoCorrect item and you'll find options for switching on and off automatic correction for just about everything short of testing the temperature of the baby's bath water.

Do make it a practice with Word, and other programs, to check out any items labelled Options or Preferences so that you can see to what extent you can tweak the way the program looks or works.

SEEING DOUBLE

Q I have Word 2. Recently I wanted to remove all single hard carriage returns and convert double carriage returns to singles, but I got into a total mess, ending up with an unreadable slab of continuous text which left me with a time-consuming manual edit to perform. Is there a way round the problem, please?

A This sounds a touch technical but, actually, it can be a common problem. The answer is to go about the solution in two stages.

Word allows you to Find and Replace hard carriage returns using the sequence ^p. What we mean by carriage returns is an end of line marker, if you like. The expression goes back to the days of manual typewriters, when you had to reach out and give the arm sticking out a hard whack to get the carriage back to the beginning of the line, at the same time cranking the platen roller up enough for you to begin typing on a new line.

If you replace all the occurrences of ^p with nothing, then you are indeed in a mess. The way round the problem goes something like this. First, replace all double ^p^p sequences with a unique set of characters, like *****. Then you can eradicate the single carriage returns. Finally, replace the ***** sequence with a single ^p. We hope you understand that!

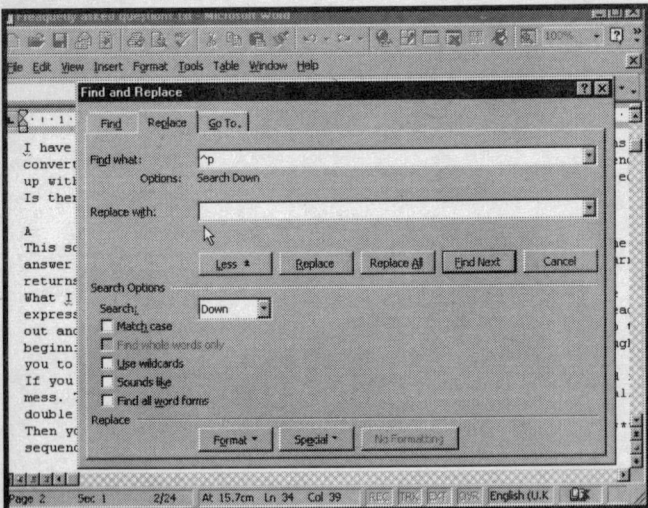

NO CD SOUND

Q I can't get any sound out of my CD player even though the volume slider is at max. Any suggestions will be greatly appreciated

A Two basic preliminary suggestions: are the speakers connected properly to the PC, or is the volume level of the speakers set at an adaquately audible setting?

However, the more likely possibility is that the cable that connects the sound card and the CD-ROM drive is loose, thus causing no sound to travel from CD to speaker.

Looking through the Win95 Resource book, it is also possible that the CD Audio MCI (Multimedia Control Interface) driver is not installed or not enabled. To see if it works go to the Multimedia option in Control Panel and click on the Advanced tab. In the Multimedia Devices list, click the plus (+) sign next to Media Control Devices.

If CD Audio Device(Media Control) appears in the list, click on it and then click Properties. In the Properties dialog box, click 'Use This Media Control Device.'

If CD Audio Device(Media Control) does NOT appear in the list, the driver is not installed. In that case:

1. Go to Add New Hardware, click No when prompted to have Windows search for your hardware, then click Next.

2. In the Hardware Types list, click Sound, Video and Game Controllers, and click Next.

3. Click Microsoft MCI in the Manufacturers list, then click CD Audio Device(Media Control) in the Models list. Click Next, then Finish.

TO SCAN OR NOT TO SCAN

Q I wonder if you can help me. I am thinking of buying a scanner but haven't got much desk space. Could you tell me if the new scanner cartridges for the Canon BJ4300 bubble jet are a good idea?

A We have tried scanner cartridges from other manufactures in the past, but not the Cannon. They are a good idea if you're short on space, but we would still recommend you find some room and go for a A4 flatbed scanner, as they are much more versatile. When it comes down to it, in the time it takes to change a cartridge you could have plugged in a flatbed, completed a scan, and then popped it under the desk, neatly out of the way.

EPROM CORRUPTION

Q Ever since my son put in a new modem (a 56K Winmodem) last Christmas, every time I boot up I get the boxed message "Your EPROM is corrupted." What does that mean? My computer works fine. Everyone I have asked about this does not seem to know either, so I just ignore it and go on my merry way. Still, I really would like to know what it means. Any answers, please?

A When the computer starts up it attempts to read all the EPROM's on any boards it finds, such as your video card's ROM for instance. In your case, it seems that there is a problem with the ROM on your modem card. This should not, however, effect the operation of your PC and if your modem still works, all is well. So, just ignore the message.

LOCATING THE CHARACTER MAP

Q A quick question regarding the character map: WHERE IS IT?!? I can't seem to find it anywhere and all my searches come to nothing! Can anyone help, please?

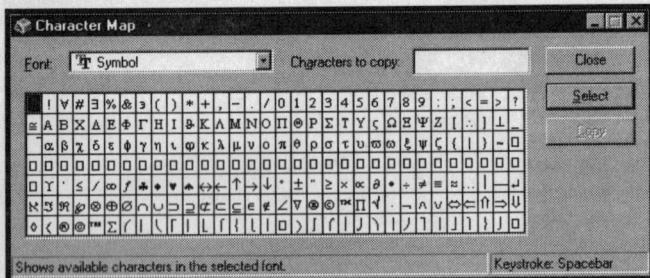

A It was probably not installed on the PC when Win 95 was installed.

No problem though. You will need the Windows 95 CD at hand.

1) Go to the Control Panel, then to Add/Remove Programs. Click on the Windows Setup tab. Windows will take few seconds to see what is installed on your machine.

2) When the list of items appear (Accessories, Communications, etc.) select the System Tools entry. Click on the Details button. Now, from this list you should find Character Map. Place a check mark next to it with a left click. Click OK.

3) Click the Apply or the OK button. Windows will now ask for the Win 95 CD so it can install Character Map. That should do the trick.

ILLEGAL IE4

Q Having recently loaded IE4, I am told that this has performed an illegal action and will terminate. With the exception of a task box, I cannot access any other program. How do I get round this, or uninstall IE4?

A We had the same problem, due, in most part, to the usual array of Win95 gremlins - one reason why it's worth upgrading to Win 98. The only way we could solve it was to delete the iexplore.exe file, re-install IE3.0 and then re-install IE4.0. This seemed to overcome whatever glitch had happened the first time around. Good luck!

WIN98 - FRESH INSTALL OR UPDATE WIN95?

Q I have just purchased Win98 and would like some feedback on whether its better to completely install Win98 and delete Win95, or go for the 'update 95 only' option.

A We have upgraded several computers in our office and found Windows 98 to be very reliable. I would go for the complete install option unless you have hard drive space to burn.

DESKTOP PROBLEMS...

Q I have a Dell dimension series PC with Windows 98. Word was not on the desktop; it was only available through Programs on the Start menu. I managed to left click and drag it from Programs to the desktop, and it's showing as a shortcut. I later discovered how to create a proper shortcut, which is what I should have done first (!), as Word is now no longer shown on the Programs list and I cannot get it back. Please can you help?

A Here's how to get it back.

1) Right click the start task bar.

2) Left click Properties

3) Left click the Start Menu Programs tab

4) Left click the Add program button, then the browse button, find your program and click on it to select it.

5) Now click Open, then the Next button

6) Now select the folder where you want the program to appear and then hit the Next button.

7) Type in a suitable title - or accept the default one - and finally click the Finished button

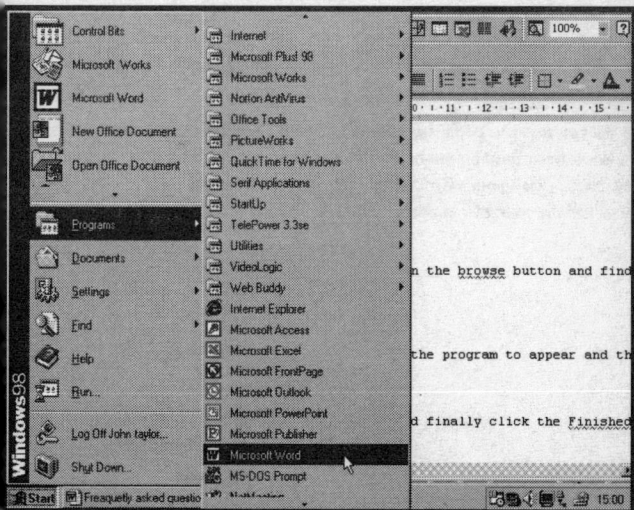

A FRESH OUTLOOK

Q I have Outlook 98 on my computer. My wife has Outlook Express on her newly bought PC in the UK (I live in Cyprus). What files do I need to email her so that my extensive address book/contacts list can be accessed by her using Outlook Express?

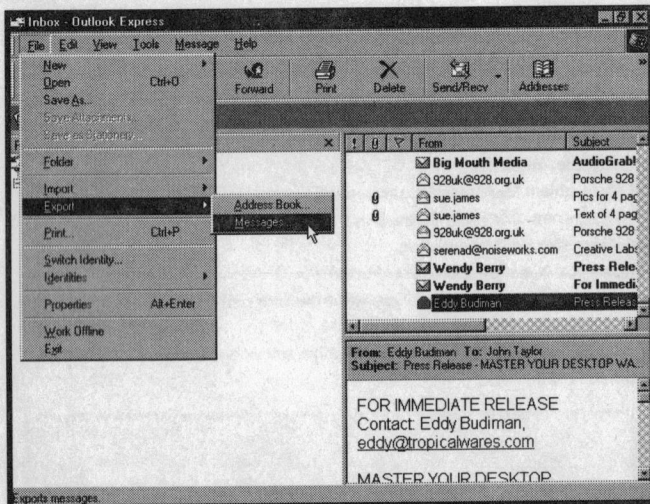

A All you need to do is use the Export Files Selection and then the Address Book from the File menu. First, export the files as Microsoft Exchange files. Next, email your wife the exported file and then all your wife has to do is use the file menu to import the files to her machine. Simple as that!

WIN98: RETRIEVING FILES CREATED IN WIN 95

Q Further to upgrading my PC to Win98, I can't retrieve my CV, which was typed in Win95. When I open my floppy disk where the CV is stored it tells me the content and title of my floppy, and I can even see the title, but double clicking doesn't open it. Help!

A You don't say what word processor you used to write your document but we haven't heard of any problems concerning reading files after a 95-to-98 upgrade. You do say your file is stored on a floppy disk. I am sure this will be the problem. Floppy disks are nowhere near as reliable as hard drives. They go wrong all the time. The disks corrupt and people often forget that the disk drive heads need cleaning. Try cleaning your disk drive heads first; you can get a cleaning kit from PC World or Dixons. Your problem does not sound like a Windows 98 problem - it's probably just a coincidence. Have you tried copying your file to your hard drive and opening your word processor first, then using File Open from the menu? It sounds like Windows may have lost its association for this type of file.

CAN'T RECEIVE IN OUTLOOK EXPRESS

Q I use Outlook Express and have just installed Office 97 with the Outlook email software packaged with it. I can send mail from it, but for some reason I cannot receive mail to it. I am asked for a POP3 Account server...what is this please?

A POP3 stands for Point Of Presence. It is the address of your email account provider. For example, here at Paragon, ours is www2.paragon.co.uk. As for your problem, it's worth contacting your Internet service provider (examples include AOL, CompuServe and Freeserve); they should be able to set up an account for you.

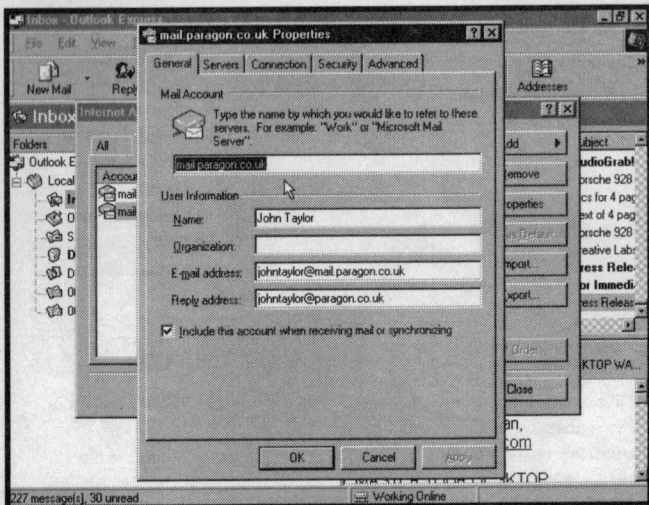

A MULTITUDE OF CD-ROM DRIVES...

Q Upon installing my CD ROM drive, I have found that in "My Computer", or under "Windows Explorer", four drives appear onscreen. I know it should be drive D: but I have D: E: F: G: showing; and yet the last drive in my config.sys is set as D: What should I do to have just one drive showing?

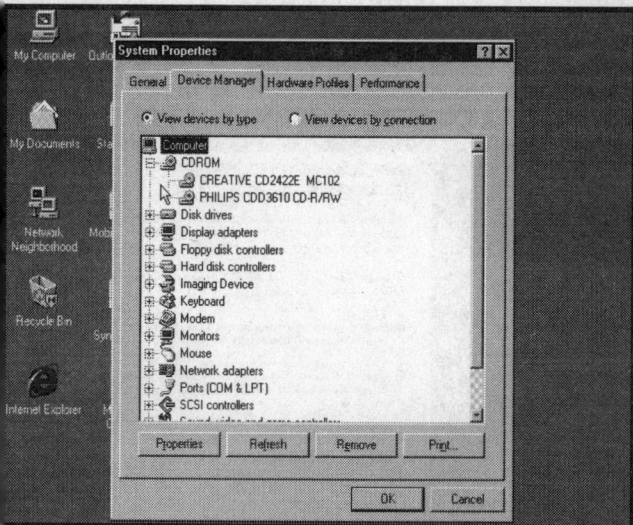

A This is a good one! To be honest, it could be any number of things. So, here goes...

It is probably unlikely but you could have a multi-session CD in your drive, and this would show up as lots of drives. Alternatively, you may have multiple drivers for your CD installed. To check this out go to the start menu, then Settings and then find the icon called System and double click it. Now click the device manager tab. Click the plus (+) next to CD-ROM and there should be only one driver. If there are more, simply remove them.

The last option I can think of is that you have a DOS driver loaded as well as a Windows one. However, Windows usually copes with this so I can't see what has gone wrong if this is the case.

DIAL UP DIALOG

Q When I open Internet Explorer, it doesn't automatically bring up my dial up connection dialog box anymore. I have set up a shortcut on my desktop to my dial up connection which I now click on to get to Internet Explorer. How do I get Internet explorer to auto dial when I open it? Why did it stop displaying the dial up connection dialog box?

A We guess that Explorer no longer thinks you have a dial up account If may have lost your account details or it could be set to a network connection. This usually happens when you install Internet software from other companies or magazine cover disks. The best thing you can do is simply re-run the connection wizard.

Internet Connection Wizard

Welcome to the Internet Connection Wizard

The Internet Connection wizard helps you connect your computer to the Internet. You can use this wizard to set up a new or existing Internet account.

○ I want to sign up for a new Internet account. (My telephone line is connected to my modem.)

○ I want to transfer my existing Internet account to this computer. (My telephone line is connected to my modem.)

○ I want to set up my Internet connection manually, or I want to connect through a local area network (LAN).

To leave your Internet settings unchanged, click Cancel.

To learn more about the Internet, click Tutorial.   [Tutorial]

[< Back] [Next >] [Cancel]

MY PC CAN'T SEE MY CD-ROM!

Q I've just installed a second hard drive - and now Windows 95 can't see it. It's been allocated an "E" letter, and I can access it in DOS, but neither Explore nor "My Computer" can see it - help, please.

A Don't panic - we've all been here before!

To see your CD-ROM in DOS you must have DOS drivers loaded from your Autoexec.bat.
Use MSCDEX.EXE to allocate your drive to a new letter.
For example:
MSCDEX [L:]
MSCDEX L: G
Alternatively, remove your DOS driver and let Windows allocate a letter automatically.
Hope this helps!

SOUND CARD COMPATIBILITY PROBLEMS

Q I have just bought a P.C. having come from an Amiga (don't laugh). Its a 350mhz P2 with 128k Ram etc., etc.

Anyway, I have been catching up on some of the great software that I have missed over the last couple of years (e.g. Settlers 2 and Duke Nukem 3D). Alas, I can't seem to get the audio to work with them, as you have to set up the sound installation yourself. It appears that my sound card is not connected the way the programme thinks it should (DMA and I/Os?) How do I find out where they are on my computer or how my sound card is configured? (Is there a menu that gives you this information? I have a Sound Vision card Yamaha OPL3-SAx.)

A The Yamaha OPL3-SAX sound card should have a CD-ROM to accompany it, which should have the relevant drivers on it and a program called "Yamaha Station". If you have installed this correctly, it should put all the information you need regarding DMA, IO, etc. in your Autoexec.bat file. If you edit this in Notepad, you will notice a line which begins "SETBLASTER=" These are your settings and you should use these in preference to the Windows' settings because they are the card's default settings and will work with all programs.

Occasionally, we have found that you need to tell some programs that it is a "SoundBlaster pro"; others prefer you to set it to "compatible-compatible". By the way, the midi port is an MPU401 on port 380, and does not work with some games.

AN APPROACH TO MAIL MERGE

Q I am trying to use mail merge to create a mailing list in Microsoft Word but my database is an Approach file, and I can't seem to do it - help, please! I've tried to convert/export the Approach file to odbc, and this it doesn't work either. I've even tried Microsoft online, but to no avail!

A Simple...when you know how. Export your file as a CSV file (Comma Delimited) and all should be well.

FILE ASSOCIATION ATTACHMENTS

Q I've been sent a WP document file as an email attachment, which was saved in Microsoft Works. I don't have this program, so when I tried to download this file I was told that it couldn't be opened. I do have MS Word, though, which can open documents saved in other WP formats. So, I went into Windows and changed the file association for Works so that it would be opened by Word. This didn't work. Is there anything else I can do (apart from asking the person to re-send the document as an .rtf or .txt file)?

A If you are using Office 97, left click File, and then Open. When the Open file dialog box comes up there will be a section called 'Files of type.' Click the arrow next to this and go down the list until you find MS Works. Now select the location in the 'Look In' section and you will be able to import it.

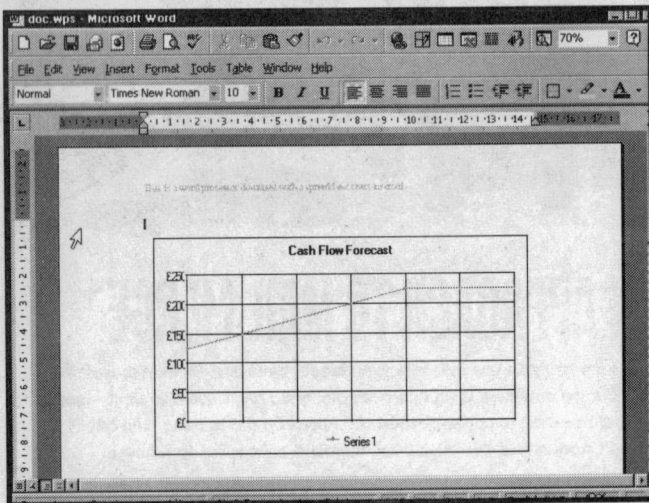

ICONS ON THE MOVE

Q Why is it that when I start my computer (Windows 95) the Icons on the Desktop do not stay in the place that I have left them?

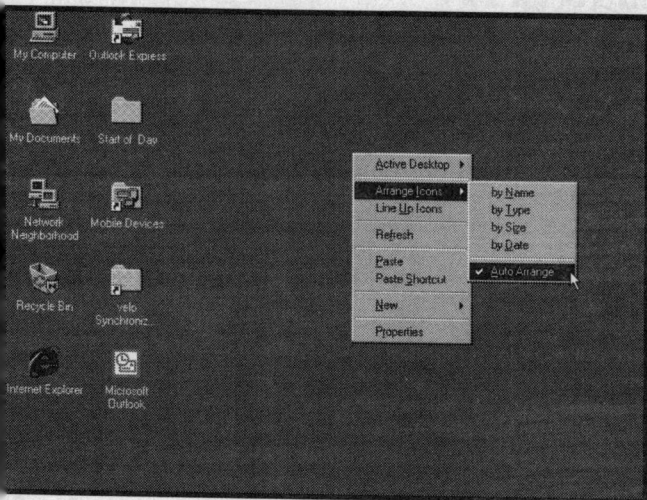

My Computer · Outlook Express · My Documents · Start of Day · Network Neighborhood · Mobile Devices · Recycle Bin · velo Synchroniz... · Internet Explorer · Microsoft Outlook

Active Desktop ▸
Arrange Icons ▸   by Name
Line Up Icons   by Type
Refresh   by Size
Paste   by Date
Paste Shortcut   ✓ Auto Arrange
New ▸
Properties

A On the Desktop right click with mouse, go to Arrange Icons on the pop-up menu and ensure Auto Arrange is NOT ticked. This should do the trick.

DIGITAL GAMEPADS AND ANALOG JOY

Q I recently bought and installed a Sidewinder gamepad to use with some of my computer games. Up until this I was using a standard 2 Button 2 Axis Joystick.

The problem is that I uninstalled the gamepad and now I can't get the gameport to recognise the original joystick configuration. I have tried uninstalling all gamepad and joystick configurations and reinstalling the original drivers, setting up a 2 axis-2 button joystick in Control Panel. The gameport tells me that all the devices are working properly, but when I try to calibrate the joystick it tells me that none are connected. Have I, by installing the digital gamepad, removed the capability for my soundcard (Yamaha DS-XG Legacy) to drive an analog joystick?

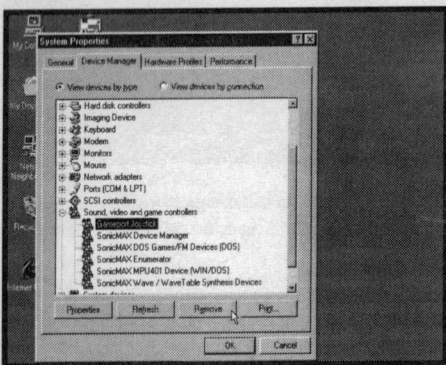

A The problem that you are having is possibly due to your joystick driver file 'Vjoyd.vxd' being corrupt. To fix this you need to go to Control panel, System, then Device Manager and remove your 'Gameport Joystick' from the section marked 'Sound, video and game controllers.' Now restart your computer.

Next, insert your Windows CD and go to Add New Hardware. Let Windows auto-detect your Gameport for you.

If it finds a driver on the C:\ drive, you should click on the Other Locations tab and tell it to look in D:\win95 (if your CD-ROM is D:\). It will now install a new joy stick driver.

Alternatively, if it finds a driver on the CD, click next and it will install the new driver.

DRIVESPACE PROBLEM

Q I recently had to remove my Windows directory to reinstall windows. My old version of Windows was 4.95a, but my newer version is 4.95b. I do not use compressed drives at the moment, but I am unable to uninstall Drivespace3 in MSPlus. It tells me the backup files are missing or that I'm using the wrong version. Is there a way around this?

A The reason you are getting this message it that you are installing a version of Plus! that was intended for use with Win95a only (Drivespace3 was an add-on for this version). Drivespace3 is included in the B version of Windows 95 on the master CD. To install Disk Compression in Win95B, go to Control Panel, Add/remove programs, and then Windows setup. In here you should see Disk Tools. Highlight this and click the Details tab. Put a tick in the box next to 'Disk compression tools' and press OK. Windows will now install Disk Compression and ask you for the Windows 95 CD-ROM to be inserted. Once this has been installed and you have restarted, you will be able to use the disk compression tools to compress your hard disk. The tools can be found in the Start menu under Programs, Accessories, System Tools. Please note, however, that Disk Compression severely slows your system down, and can cause data corruption and premature hard-drive wear.

DEFAULT PROBLEMS WITH IE4

Q I recently completed a full version upgrade to Win98 from Win95. When I opened up Internet Explorer 4 for the first time I was asked if I wanted to make this my default browser. Obviously, having not used IE in any version before, I wanted to try it out first before choosing, and therefore clicked no! Having tried it out I decided to keep it but the dialog box for this question has not appeared since. Now I'm running IE4 and my system thinks my default browser is Netscape. I have trawled through the usual files but can't find the switch to change my default. This is causing problems with ICQ, Net Meeting, and even opening attachments from emails.

A When you open Internet Explorer, go to the Internet options screen in the view menu. Now click on the Programs tab at the top and you will see a radio box without a tick in it. To tell IE to check if it is the default browser, just click this box to tick it and press Apply. After you have restarted your computer and loaded up IE you will be asked if you want IE as your default browser, and you can now answer with a resounding 'yes' this time.

SCANDISK KEEPS ON RUNNING...

Q Though I have got no other program running, Scandisk gives me the message: "SCANDISK has restarted 10 times." I know that quitting some running applications might solve the problem, but not when I haven't got any applications running! This means that I cannot defragment my drive as the drive cannot be checked for errors. What can I do?
My system software is Win98, upgraded from Win95.

A This is because there is a program (or programs) already running which is accessing the hard drive. Close all programs except Explorer by pressing the Ctrl, Alt and Del keys on the keyboard simultaneously. Highlight a program and then click the button marked End Task.

Here, though, is another possible solution: try using Scandisk under DOS.

1) Shutdown your computer and turn it back on.

2) During the boot processor, hit the 'F8' key to bring up the Windows boot options screen.

3) Select 'DOS prompt.'

4) From 'C:\' type 'scandisk' and hit Enter (for example: c:\scandisk).

5) When Scandisk is finished you can type 'win' and hit Enter to go into windows...

6) ...or, if you're at the 'c:\' prompt, just hit the reset button on your computer.

HOMEPAGE HORRORS & PASSWORD PUZZLES

Q My husband and I recently bought a computer. I 'accidentally' made a few pages disappear but my homepage is the one thing I really don't want and I'm having difficulty getting rid of it. Also, when I log on, Windows asks for the password and when I want to access a Wizard it won't let me because it says 'password incorrect.' No one seems to know how to fix this. Please help.

A If you are using Internet Explorer, go to the View menu (if you have IE4), or the Tools menu (if you have IE5). Then go to Internet Options - here, you can change your homepage to whatever you want.

If, on the other hand, you are using Netscape Navigator, you should go to the Edit menu, click preferences and then you'll be able to change your homepage from the Navigator Category.

You are a bit vague on which Wizard you need to get into but, if you have forgotten the Windows password, open the 'System.ini' file, which can be found inside the C:\Windows folder, then go right to the bottom. You should be able to see a list of passwords. Delete all of the entries in here and you will be able to enter a new password when you next restart your computer.

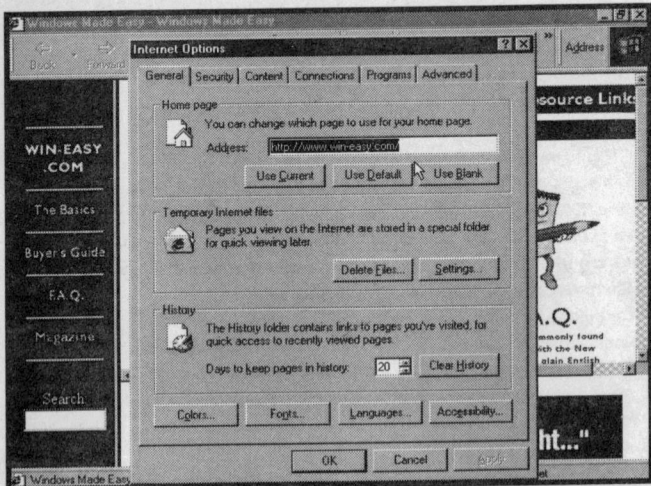

TAKING A SCREEN DUMP

Q How do I print the whole screen on my printer under Windows 95 or 98. I though you had to press Shift+Printscreen, but all my attempts haven't really come to much.

A First, press Print Scrn. Then, open a new Paint document and press Ctrl+V to paste the picture. You will be able print it from there.

CRASH

Q I bought a PC recently and ever since it keeps locking up. When it locks up (crashes), all different types of window open up all over the screen and I have to keep resetting. The mouse pointer also stops. I've tried everything, even a few things from the help desk at PC Direct, but I'm still locking up.

A Sadly, the problem could be anything. It could be a problem with Windows, in which case a full install will solve the problem. Or, if you're running Win95, try upgrading to 98 as the problem could stem from a hardware clash. If this is the case, you should find that the Windows 98 installation is rather nifty at sorting out resource problems. If you have any add-on cards connected to your PC take them out and put them back one at a time until you find the card causing the initial problem. Lastly, it could be one of your programs that is causing all the difficulties, so make sure you are running a clean computer at all times.

PLEASE HOLD...

DIAL UP CONNECTION WINDOW

Q When I log onto my PC (Windows 98) I get not one, not two, but three dial up connection windows. Then, after closing them, about a minute later I get another. I wouldn't mind, but I don't want any prompt at all when I log on! Any ideas as to how I can stop this ?

A Something in your Win98 startup file needs an Internet connection. Not all Internet applications cause this. For example, AOL and ICQ do not log you on but wait for you to manually connect. The most likely place to look is: In the bottom right-hand corner where the clock is, verify that none of your applications are causing the dialup hang ups.

Alternatively, try this solution:

1) Right click 'Start'

2) Left click 'Explore'

3) Locate the 'c:\Windows\Start Menu'

4) Left click the 'Start Menu' folder

5) Look at each program in the folder. Chat, Automatic updates, etc. applications may be the cause of the dialup during your WIN98 bootup.

MICROSOFT PUBLISHER

Q After re-installing Publisher it now won't run, but shows a note: "MSPub caused invalid page fault in Module Kernel32.DLL at 013f:bff857c7 (etc.)" I have copied over another copy of the that library, just in case, but I still get the message. Strangely, the setup for Publisher proceeds well and tells me it has been installed correctly. Help, please!

A We have seen page faults arise when there is a application, such as MSPub, which demands a different display configuration than your system currently has. This might be worth a try: Make sure your video adapter is capable of handling True colour. If you're running a Pentium and you have at least 2MB of memory for video RAM, then you're probably OK.

RELOCATING FAVOURITES

Q How do you relocate your favourites to another computer?

A We mainly use Netscape, but the procedure should be the same for Internet Explorer.

1) Go to the directory C:\windows\favourites
2) Right click Favourites and left click Copy.
3) Go to A:\
4) Right click the 'a' folder and left click paste.

You now have the favourites on a floppy disk, so just use similar steps to put it on the other PC.

When you put it on the other machine, you will be asked you if you want your new favourites to replace the previous favourite folder. Answer yes.

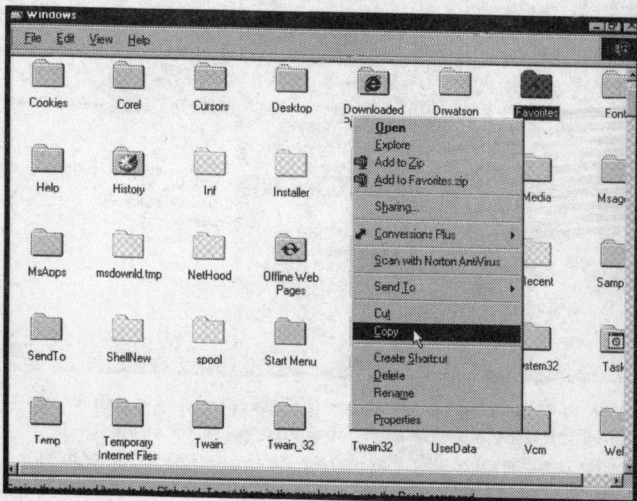

TAKE OUT THE TRASH

Q I recently loaded some files onto my hard disk from a magazine cover disk. I then deleted them by sending them to the recycle bin and emptying it. However, upon trying to empty it now, I get this message: "Cannot delete _KYTP: Make sure that the correct path and filename are specified." When I open the recycle bin, there is nothing there, but the icon shows that there is something inside. I have tried creating a new folder, renaming it to _KYT_P: but Windows (95) won't let me. Can I delete the recycle bin altogether and create a new one? Or, can I get rid of this non-existent file through DOS?

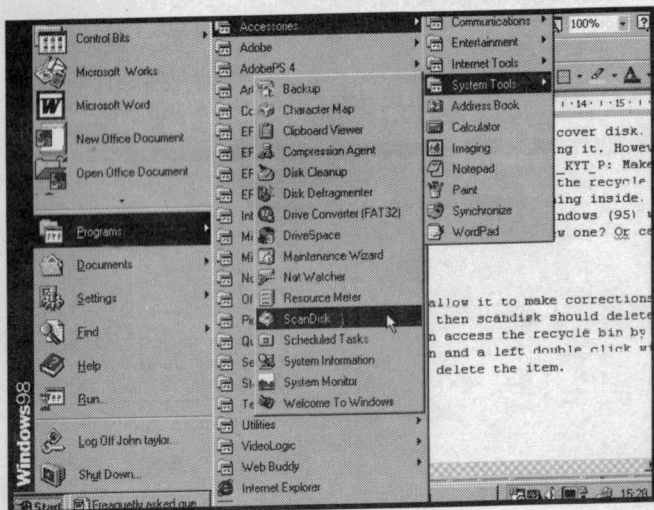

A We would run Scandisk and allow it to make corrections to your file system. If it is just a erroneous file, then Scandisk should delete it.

If the file is still present after that, you can access the recycle bin by exploring your C: drive to find the recycle bin, and a left double click will open the contents. From here you can attempt to delete the item.

If you want to use DOS, then it's in C:\recycled.

WHAT IS BETA SOFTWARE?

Q I would like to know what does it means when somebody says "The BETA version of software?" What's BETA?

A 'Beta' is short for Betaware. Betaware is a pre-release of software or hardware for users like us to try out. It is usually free, but the catch is the issuing company would normally like you to provide feedback on any problems you may have with the software or hardware. The Betaware allows the company to fine tune their product before releasing a version for sale on the market. Here's some other product version-types you may like to know:

Freeware - a gift from the owner to the user, but normally the owner would like donations…or just a kindly thank you.

Shareware - a permission-to-try software or hardware which is normally sold for free. After the trial period you are expected to pay for the license or discontinue using the item.

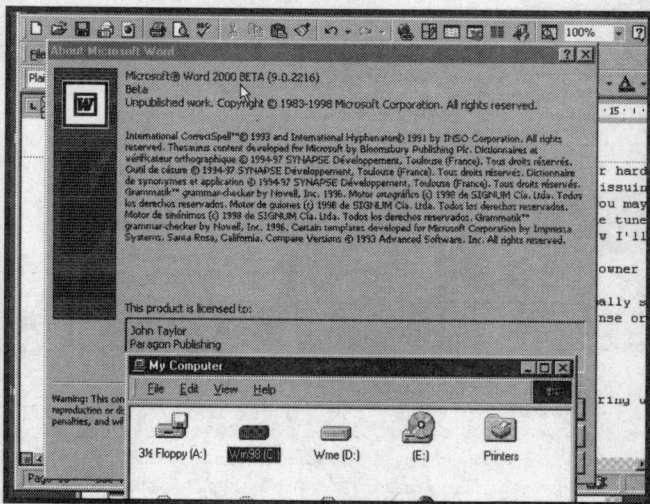

CREATING ICONS

Q I have tried to create icons, as featured in issue five of *Windows Made Easy*, but when I bring up the desktop properties, there is no effects tab. Where will it be?

A It looks like you have an early copy of Windows 95 which did not have an effects tab. You will need to upgrade to Windows 98 or add Microsoft Plus to your Windows system. There are also maintenance updates available from http://www.microsoft.com

BROWSING IN THE RIGHT ORDER

Q When using the run command I find that if I use the browse option to try and locate files on my computer, they appear in descending order by name. I can manage to place them in the correct order by clicking the Details button and using the name column, but this only works as a temporary measure. Could you please point me in the direction of the properties setting that will permanently select the sort order?

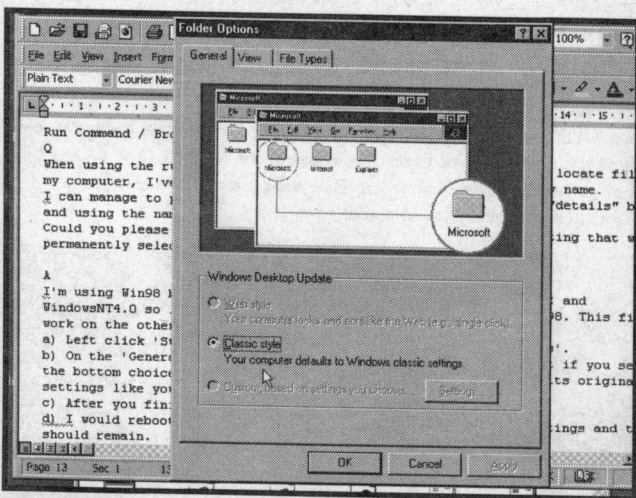

A We're using Win98 but this fix may work on other versions:

1) Left click Start. Select Settings and then Folder Options.
2) On the General tab you should have three choices. It is best if you select the bottom choice, otherwise it Windows will default to its original settings, as you have mentioned.
3) After you finish with the settings, click OK.
4) We would reboot Windows now, and then make any additional settings - they should remain.

SWOLLEN ICONS

Q I had a look at the Windows 98 Tutorial CD-ROM (I've got Win95), and since then my desktop icons, etc., have swollen in size, almost as though I'd zoomed in. I've tried to change settings in My Computer, but to no avail. I want to pan out, but there's no response. Any ideas?

A I think you're saying you want to resize your desktop.

1) Find a blank space on your desktop and right click; you will see a pop-up menu.
2) Left click Properties.
3) Choose the Settings tab.
4) On the bottom-right, you will see a box named Screen Area. Inside this box is a slide bar enabling you to adjust the size of the desktop. Click OK and take a look at the other tabs, just so you know what your options are.
5) Its best if you reboot you computer now.

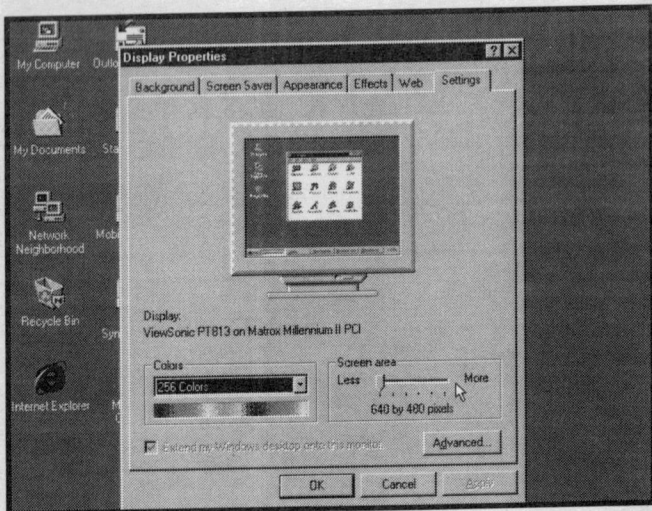

IN THE OUT TRAY

Q I would like to remove items from my Win98 system tray. Is there a way to do that from within Windows or do I have to use a third party program?

A There are several ways to remove items from the system tray:

1) Double click them and close them down.
2) Press Ctrl, Alt and Del keys simultaneously, select the program then choose End task.

Here is a more permanent solution:

1) Look in the startup folder, which can be found C:\windows\Start Menu. Delete any shortcuts you find there.
2) Look in the win.ini file for the lines

load=

run=

...they should be blank like this.

3) Finally, though not recommended for complete beginners, search the registry file for the program name using the REG Edit command.

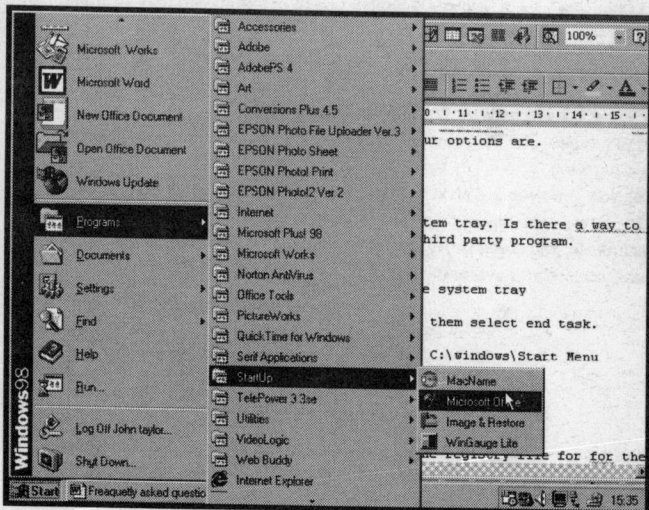

RE-FORMAT THE HARD DISK?

Q My computer came with Win98 pre-installed, so I didn't have the original CD and I wasn't registered. However, I now have the Win98 CD (full version) and want to delete everything from my hard disk - programs, operating system...everything, in fact! - and install Win98 from the beginning. Is this possible? If it is feasible, how exactly do I go about it?

A To be honest, it may not be worth the hassle. But, if you must...

Give yourself about six hours. This is not a easy process and you may encounter significant problems along the way. Still, if you wish to continue, these instructions assume you are not running disk compression (DriveSpace3).

1) Reboot your computer into DOS mode.
2) Type 'fdisk' and press Enter.
3) You should choose large hard drive support.
4) Choose option 4, which tells you exactly how many partitions you have.
5) Press ESC to exit.
6) Choose option 3, which will enable you to delete the primary DOS partition along with any others.
7) Once option 4 no longer shows any partitions, then your hard drive is empty.
8) Create a new primary DOS partition using option 1.
9) You should use 100% on the DOS partition - unless, that is, you want a second partition
10) Now you need a disk in the floppy drive (normally a:) which will tell the CD-ROM to read the Win98 CD. Note that some systems read the CD-ROM first, regardless. You can also try rebooting with the CD in the drive and see if the installation starts automatically.

WORD: END OF THE LINE

Q I have Windows 95 and Word 7. In some, but not all, files when I draw a line across a page using the short line and immediately after the last dash hit Enter, the dotted line turns to a solid line which I am unable to erase. However, if I leave a space after the last dash and then press Enter, the dotted line does not change. I should emphasise again that this only happens in some files. Have you any idea how to stop this happening ?

A Word 7 wants to help so much it ends up being a pain in neck sometimes. Disable Auto Correct - that should prevent this from happening again.

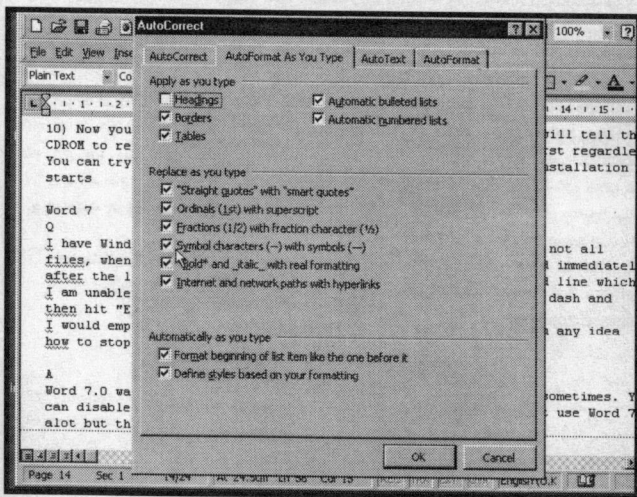

COBOL - IS IT WORTH IT?

Q I am about to embark on a change of career, and I'm thinking of learning the computer language COBOL. Is this a good starting point, and if not, what recommendations can you give me.

Also, are there any good training aids which could assist me on my quest? I have made inquiries with a company called Computeach, who offer me the freedom of learning at home at my own pace - but I would still appreciate your own opinion on the subject.

A We would recommend ANSI C and then you could roll over into C++. You should be able to get a book on ANSI C and also a C++ compiler that will comply with ANSI C. To get started in programming, we would recommend a 'Programming in C' style course to get you into the swing of things and get to grips with the basics in a hands-on environment.

If you are considering going into programming, it's often a good idea to pick two languages to specialise in. The second we would recommend would be Visualbasic, or another similar to it. The idea behind this language is to get you in a position to be able to create business applications with as little keying (in other words, hassle) as possible. Visualbasic offers programming by example, and can save you a lot of time.

But, back to your first question. What's so wrong with COBOL, then? To be blunt, we have much easier and more productive methods of creating business applications.

MISSING SETUP

Q I run an IBM Thinkpad which I recently upgraded to 4.2 GB Drive, 48 Meg RAM, and so on, and I run Windows 95, MSOffice Pro, Publisher, etc. Recently, when I reach the end of booting up, I am confronted with the legend: "Cannot find the file SETUP.EXE (or one of its components). Make sure the path and filename are correct and that all required libraries are present." I click OK and then up pops "Cannot load SETUP.EXE specified in WIN.INI file - make sure it exists or remove the ref in the WIN.INI file." Then it completes loading and everything seems to work OK. I peeked into the WIN.INI file and the only reference I could find was: RUN=C:\IBMAV95\STARTTIM.EXE, G:\BRANDING\SETUP.EXE. (G is my CD Drive). I tried inserting a colon in front of the SETUP.EXE, but to no avail - on re-booting, the notice came up as usual. The only thing I can think it might be is a Font I copied over. Any ideas please

A We think you're pretty much on the right track. Here are some ideas which might help you further.

1) You may have to put a space between the : and the line in order for windows to understand you don't want to run the item. I normally use REM (followed by a space), then the original line. See the example below (note that I don't want PBKEY to be run, so I REM'd it out).

[windows]
load=
rem run=C:\WINDOWS\SYSTEM\cmmpu.exe C:\PBKEY\PBKEY.EXE
Beep=yes
NullPort=None
BorderWidth=3
CursorBlinkRate=530
DoubleClickSpeed=452
Programs=com exe bat pif
Documents=
KeyboardDelay=2
KeyboardSpeed=31
ScreenSaveActive=0
ScreenSaveTimeOut=120
device=Brother MFL Printer,BRFAX96,COM4:

2) It's probably not a good idea for the Win ini to point to a file on your G: drive, because the specific CD may not always be in the drive. You may be booting your computer without the relevant CD in the drive.

3) While in the Win ini you can use 'SEARCH' 'FIND' at the top of the edit window to type in 'Setup.exe' and it will find all the setup.exe's in the file.

OUTLOOK DEMONS

Q IS it possible to use MS Outlook with my Demon connection and if so how do I set about it?

A An easy way, at least in theory, is to open Outlook and go to File, Import, Mail, Account Settings, and then change the relevant options there. If this brings no luck then try the following steps:

1) Get the following information from your current email program.
a) Login name,
b) Password,
c) Email address,
d) Domain,
e) Mail server (POP, IMAP or SMTP),
f) Incoming mail,
g) Outgoing mail.

2) Open Outlook and it should ask you for what it needs to know, so just fill in the blanks of what you know and then try it out. This will not affect your current email program.

3) If not, then go to Tools, Accounts, Mail and then Add.

NO CALCULATOR AND PAINT!

Q The Calculator AND Paint programs seem to have disappeared since I installed Internet Explorer 4 on my system. I have perused the Windows 95 disc so that I may re-install, but cannot see either of them. I would certainly like to include Calculator again but, as I have Coral Draw 8 is it worth going to the trouble of putting Paint back?

A The Paint application is your default .bmp viewer, so you will definitely want that for sure. Use the find function in your Start menu to search files or folders on your primary drive (C) and then type in 'mspaint' and left click Find Now. If you see the Paint icon then you can left click it and drag it onto your desktop.

If you still can't find it, then go to Start, Settings, Control Panel, Add/Remove programs and Windows setup. Double click Accessories and make sure there is a check mark in the boxes for Paint and Calculator. Click OK to finish.

ERROR MESSAGE

Q Often, when I switch on my computer, I receive the following message:

"While initialising device IOS: Error: and I/O subsystem driver failed to load. Either a file in the .\iosubsys subdirectory is corrupt, or the system is low on memory."

I've emptied the Temp file of anything I don't use and scanned and defragged. There's plenty of memory left. I've also had an 'error' message about incomplete installation, but as I didn't install my system, I don't know what to do about that. The problem might not occur for some weeks, but when it does I might have to re-start up to six or eight times. When I get an error message, how do I find out what the problem is and how to solve it? Is this a major problem?

A The IO subsystem contain the instructions that direct each part of the computer to prevent traffic jams. We have notice similar problems to yours when we're using a SCSI device. If you have any external devices, they could be causing the problem so you might want to try disconnecting them one-by-one until you know they are safe.

NO HELP WITH WORDPERFECT HELP

Q When trying to access the WordPerfect Helpfile I get a message telling me that file Wdph8.hlp has not been installed and to tick the Help for WordPerfect check box to activate it. When I open this window I find that the check box is already ticked. What more can I do?

A It sounds like the help files were erased to save on hard drive space. Do you have any programs that delete unnecessary files? The easiest thing to do is to reload the whole program and make sure the help files are selected for installation.

LOST PROGRAM WORRIES

Q I have copied data from the Address section of Lotus Organiser to a formatted floppy disk successfully, but when trying to open or print this data from it, I get "Program Not Found. Org 32 exe program needed for opening files of type Lotus organiser 97 File, and cannot be located". I have Windows 98 and all of Lotus Smartsuite 97 software installed. Can you tell me how I can retrieve the data from my floppy?

A I suggest that you don't copy you information to the floppy disk. Use Save As in the file menu and then save your data to the floppy disk. This way you know the right file is on the disk.

Also, when you come to open the file, open it from within the program. Run Lotus Organizer first then go to the file menu and select open. Then change to the floppy disk and select your file.

DELETING A SCREEN SAVER

Q I downloaded a screen saver from a Web site and, after looking at it, decided that I did not want it. I have tried to find where the file is, but cannot locate it. I have tried the "find file" search and have looked in Windows Explorer - but I cannot trace what folder/file the screen savers are located in. Can you please tell me where I should look (and how to get there)?

A Screen savers have the extension SCR, so use Find from the Start button menu, and, in the file name box, type: *.scr. A list of screen savers will be found. Now select and delete the file you are looking for.

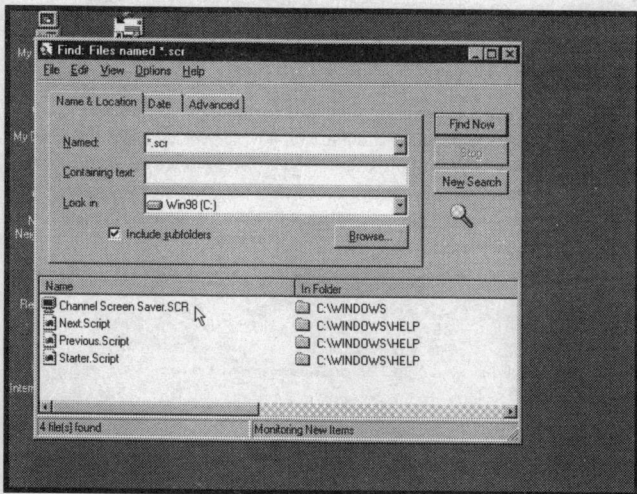

PROBLEMS WITH OUTLOOK EXPRESS

Q I am having problems when I try to send an email through Outlook Express with attachments, or when I reply back to an email that someone has forwarded me. If I create a new message or receive messages there are no problems; the error only occurs when I am replying or sending attachments. This problem seems to be happening in Outlook 98 also.

We are currently running a Packard Bell Pentium 486 (60mhz), 24ram, 2.1gig hd (we have 1.4gig remaining), an external Diamond 56k modem and Outlook 98. We also have on our system Windows 95B. Could you please advise why this error is occurring and what we can do to rectify the problem?

Note: I have also copied and pasted the settings in the control panel for email.

A First, downloading onto a removable disk is a false sense of security. As soon as the Freeware is executed it can write to your hard disk. The best rule is to run your virus check after downloading but before executing it. There are also virus protection applications specifically for downloading on the market. Secondly, you could go here: **C:\WINDOWS\Recent** and erase the contents whilst keeping the folder.

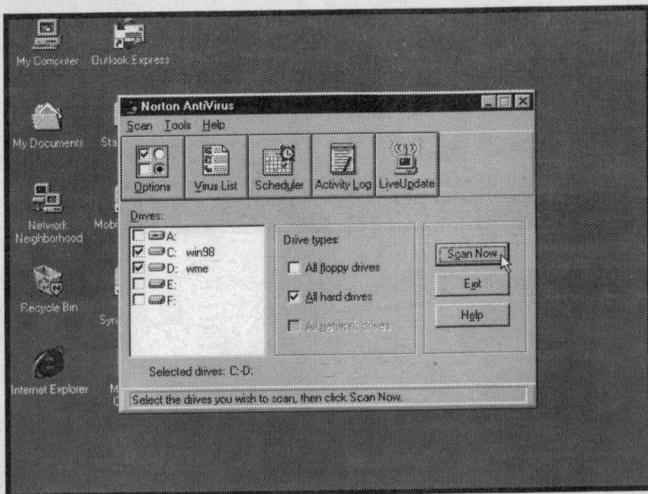

PRIVATE FOLDERS

Q I have Windows 95 version B. Both my son and I use the PC. I am about to do some work that I don't want him to be able to get at. However, I don't want to put passwords on for logging on, etc., just for a folder. Or is there some other way of stopping people from reading the folder, or files within that folder? Any suggestions would be welcome!

A We've thought this long and hard, but there is not a way to do it unless you setup another drive and upgrade to a server based system. Sorry!

PHANTOM FONTS

Q I like to email my friend using different fonts, sometimes with several different fonts within the same message. I have discovered that my efforts are often in vain as many of the fonts turn back into the default font en-route. Yet email from the same friend arrives using all the same fonts she sent it with. We have tried various methods but are stumped. PLEASE could you help ?

A Email can normally be sent with a format or without a format. Your email client may not be set to send formatted notes. Nonetheless, there are usually a few choices of format types. You might try running the same email client and, if you already are, checking the format settings; ie mime, HTML, or text.

DRIVE DISASTER

Q My floppy drive reports "disk write protected" when it is not protected. Why?

A The simple answer is that sometimes Windows just gets stuck and seizes up. Restart your computer and everything should be fine.

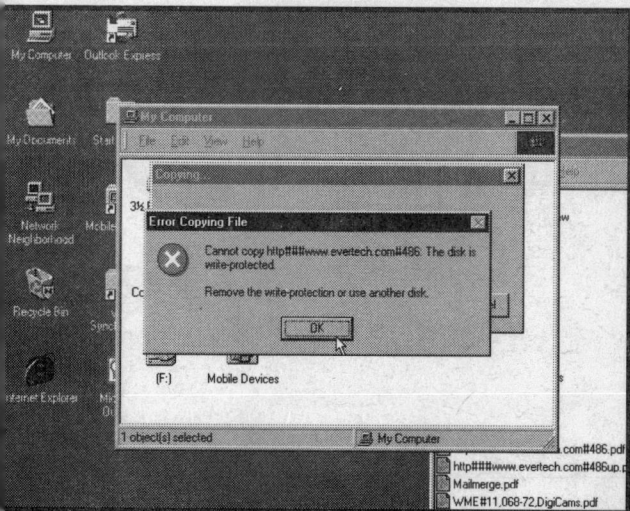

SENDING SCANS VIA EMAIL

Q I have a Black Widow scanner. My ISP is BT Click Free. My email is web-based. Try as I might, I can't send scanned photos via e-mail. Can you help ?

A If you're able to scan photographs to your hard drive, or a floppy drive, then maybe the web-based email you use does not allow you to attach items. For instance, with 'Hotmail' you're limited to about half a megabyte.

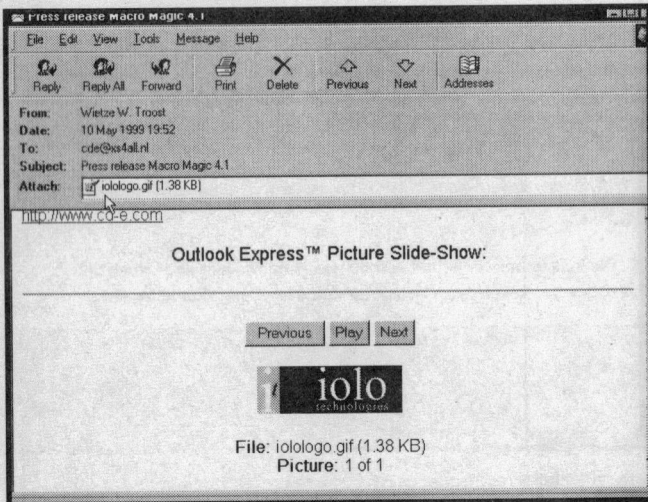

```
Press release Macro Magic 4.1

File  Edit  View  Tools  Message  Help

Reply  Reply All  Forward    Print   Delete   Previous   Next   Addresses

From:     Wietze W. Troost
Date:     10 May 1999 19:52
To:       cde@xs4all.nl
Subject:  Press release Macro Magic 4.1
Attach:   iolologo.gif (1.38 KB)
```
http://www.co-e.com

Outlook Express™ Picture Slide-Show:

Previous | Play | Next

iolo
technologies

File: iolologo.gif (1.38 KB)
Picture: 1 of 1

FONT FURY

Q I have installed some fonts from my A drive, but when I am working on a document and choose to use one of them, my computer keeps going to look for it in the A drive. If it does pick the font up it will usually be a different format to what it should be. HELP!
PS I'm running windows 95

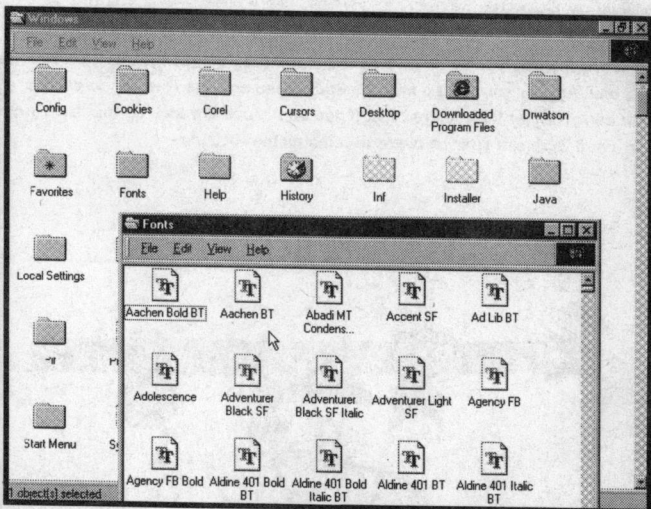

A To install fonts on your computer all you need to do is copy the fonts from your floppy drive to your hard drive in this location:
C:\windows\fonts
When you copy the fonts, Windows will check to see if they are valid. I suggest that you recopy the fonts to the above directory.

STARTUP NON-STARTER

Q When I switch on my machine everything starts up fine, but after a few minutes, a little message appears which tells me there is a startup problem and a required DLL (WDIR32.DLL) cannot be found. The only option with this message is to click OK, which I do. The message then disappears and everything works fine. I've no idea where this DLL should be, or what it is. Please can you help?

A I'm assuming you must have added a new program recently or deleted one. Anyway you can go into the Start menu and use Find File to search your computer for the required file. If you don't have any luck do that then you may need to reload your software to reinstall the .DLL file.

GETTING RID OF A PASSWORD

Q Can I get rid of the Welcome to Windows Logon window that requests my password? If so, how? I never wanted it in the first place, but I entered a password before realising I did not need it and can find no way to get out of it now. Please help!

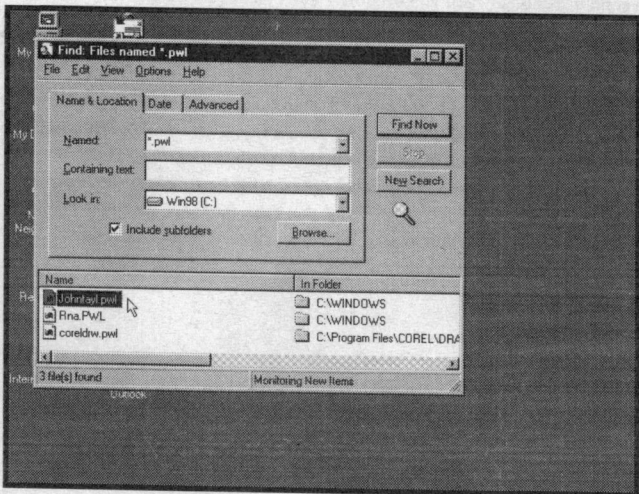

A First click on the Start button. Now go to Find and then Find Files and Folders. Select 'look in c:' Type *.pwl in the box marked name. Now click on your password file that comes up in the list box and delete it. Next time you start Windows, you will be asked for a password - do not enter one!

SAVING & SENDING WITH WORD

Q I am running Win95, series B, on my PC. I use Word97 to produce documents which include pictures/clipart and text. I set the document correctly and then want to save and send to recipients. Is there any way to save/send those documents without the Word window/toolbars being sent also? I wanted to send a greetings 'card' the other day and I just could not get rid of the surrounding paraphernalia. Is there any way of doing so?

A The tool bar is special to your Word configuration, so if the receiving party does not have the tool bar selected then they shouldn't see a tool bar. Anyway, you should be able to Save As "filename.jpg," or .html or any other file type that will use another application to view the item. Once you select Save As under the File menu, you will see a box with the file types in it. Just select a file type other than .Doc, .txt, or .rtf that you think (or know) the receiving computer will be able to read. Normally, everyone can view .html types.

DVD

Q I recently loaded the Windows 98 disc (which was supplied with my computer) and clicked 'Browse this disc.' I clicked on Drivers and came across DVD drivers. Now, in theory, can I pop along to my local video shop, rent a DVD film and play it on my computer? I would be grateful if you could help me as I was thinking of purchasing a DVD machine.

A You must have a CD-ROM drive that specifically states DVD on the front door. If your computer has DVD then most likely it has been configured for use. The drivers you found on the Win98 disk are good, valid drivers but you must have a DVD-CD-ROM drive in order to use those drivers.

FULL-SCREEN DISPLAY

Q I cannot get a full screen display on my monitor. There is no problem vertically but, horizontally, there is a black border each side of the screen about half an inch wide. At first I thought it was the monitor, so I tried another one. I had the same result. I have tried adjusting the monitor controls, every screen resolution and refresh rate, all to no effect. I am running Win95 on a Pentium P60. My graphics card is a Videologic Graffixstar 600 <2MB), which I only put in a month ago. My display is currently set at hi-colour 800x600 56hz. So, what's wrong.

A Are you running Win95 PLUS? PLUS has settings to stretch the desktop. Our Sony monitor has an adjustment which will actually let me put part of the view off screen so I can get rid of all borders. Therefore, you might want to give PLUS a try.

CHANGING COLOURS

Q I have two separate pieces of software installed on my computer. One requires 256 colours to operate, and the other will only operate on 16 bit colour. At the moment I am constantly changing the display settings and restarting my computer every time I want to switch between the two programs. Is there an easier way around this?

A Win98 has the option to not restart, but just change the colour instead. Some programs don't like this method, but it might be worth a try.

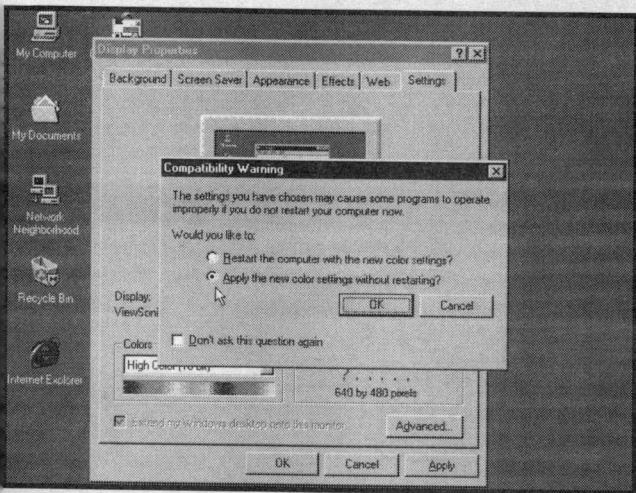

GETTING RID OF TASK SCHEDULER

Q I have the Task Scheduler icon on the taskbar in the lower-right corner of the screen and I don't use it at all. I tried to remove it from the screen, but it just won't go. Help!

A Open up Scheduled Tasks, via the Programs/Accessories/System Tools route. In the Scheduled Tasks window, click on Advanced and then select 'Stop Using Task Scheduler' from the menu. This should make the icon disappear completely.

Alternatively, here's another solution if you have Win98, as Win95 would let you do the above, but 98 is set up a little differently. Here is the fix for Win98: Go through the following commands and menus:
Start/Programs/accessories/system tools/system information/Tools/System Configuration Utility/Startup. Here you will see all the applications which may be started by Windows. Just uncheck the one you don't want, which, in this case, is the Scheduler.

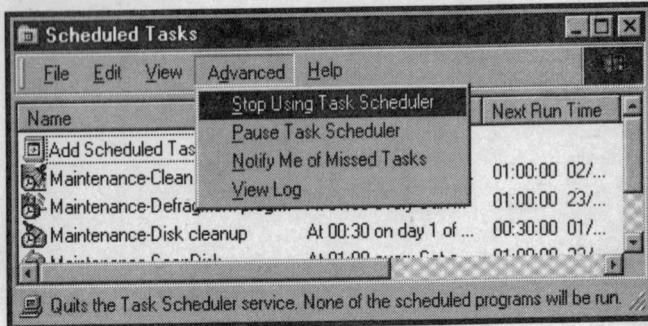

FOLDER VIEWS

Q My Windows Explorer is refusing to remember individual folder settings. There are some folders I want to display as a Web page, and some I want to display as a normal page. When I bring up the menu bar and click on 'display as Web page' so that the check mark disappears, the page reverts to a normal view. If I go into another folder and then come back, the page is displayed as a Web page again. I have checked to see that 'remember each folder's view settings' has a tick against it, and it has.

I have run Scandisk and Disk Defragmenter, and the file checker programs on Windows 98, but to no avail. I noticed this problem shortly after I downloaded Internet Explorer 5 from the Windows Website. Could that be anything to do with it? I've reset the folder options and tried every possible combination, but the system still refuses to remember the settings for each folder. I've unchecked the 'remember each folder's view' box, re-booted, put a check in it again and re-booted once more, but it still refuses to remember each folder's views.

A Make sure you have the following configuration:

Go to Start, Settings, Folder options, and on the General tab, you should have the bottom hole selected as such: 'Custom, based on setting you choose.'

Left click the Settings button and read through the options. Note that a few of the choices can have a default Web effect, so read carefully.

SAVING PHOTO IMAGES

Q I've been trying to scan old photos and save them on disk using Corel Print House Magic. The problem is when I choose Save As and try to store the image. All I get when I try to retrieve from the floppy is a window with the words 'RAW DATA BITMAP.' Where am I going wrong?

A It sounds like you are not selecting the type of file you want to save, such as .TIF .GIF or .JPG, for example. Look for a box with a down arrow and click on it. Then, click on the file type of your choice. Also, save your picture file to your hard drive first, as the picture may actually be too big to fit on a floppy.

INSTALLING MOUSE DRIVERS IN DOS

```
Autoexec.bat - Notepad                              _ □ X
File  Edit  Search  Help
rem  - By Windows 98 Network for Netware Upgrade -
C:\WINDOWS\lsl.com
rem  - By Windows 98 Network for Netware Upgrade -
C:\WINDOWS\3C5X9.com
rem  - By Windows 98 Network for Netware Upgrade -
C:\WINDOWS\odihlp.exe
rem  - By Windows 98 Network for Netware Upgrade -
C:\WINDOWS\ipxodi.com
c:\maestro.com
c:\windows\command\mouse.com|
```

Q I have recently bought some games that run best from DOS. I installed them and tried to run them, but got an error saying that there was no mouse driver installed. I contacted the helpline for the game and the chap I spoke to emailed me the mouse driver and told me what to do. I keep buying this type of game and every time I want to install one I have to go into Windows Explorer, copy the mouse driver to the directory of the game I'm trying to run and, when I start it up from DOS, I have to type 'mouse' first.

Is there any way I can install this mouse driver in DOS so that it is available for any future games I install?

A Yes. You can get the mouse driver to load every time you turn on your computer and you will only need one copy of the mouse driver. I assume you have mouse.com.

1) Go to the Start button, then Programs, Accessories and finally Notepad.

2) Double click on Notepad.

3) Go to File, then Open.

4) Change the directory to c:\

5) In the File Name box, type: autoexec.bat

6) Move the cursor to the end of the list of commands and type: c:\windows\command\mouse.com. Now save the changes.

7) Make sure a copy of mouse.com is in c:\windows\command. If not, copy it to this location.

8) Now shut down your computer, turn it off, and then turn it on again.

CONVERTING PHOTOS FROM JPG TO BITMAP

Q I have got a great photo of my two lads on floppy, but they are in jpg format. How do I change them to bitmap and put them on my wallpaper with Windows 95?

A If you open the jpg using Paint, which is included in the Accessories component of Windows, you can save it as a bitmap and set it as desktop wallpaper from there (the Set as Wallpaper option is listed in the File menu).

ACTIVE MOVIE CONTROL

Q When I try to open certain AVI or AU file attachments, I get a message which says "No combination of filters could be found to render the stream." Any advice please?

A Make sure you have the newest Windows Media Player. I can't think of a AVI filter that is not included with the Windows Media Player. You can download it for free at: http://www.microsoft.com.

SLOW SCANNER

Q My Devcom 4830 pro worked fine on my old Win95 desktop, but since getting a Win98 notebook, the scanner refuses to acknowledge the fact I have the parallel port set to EPP (even though it is.) It consequently will only scan if the PP is at the normal setting, and it takes light years to complete a scan. I've tried re-installing, but found no joy whatsoever. Is it Win98, the scanner or the computer?

A Try checking the CMOS setting. When you switch on your computer, hit the ESC or DEL key (which ever your computer tells you) to enter Setup. Then, look around for the page with the com and LPT ports. Now make sure that the port is set to EPP.

EURO BLUES

Q I'd like to use the Euro symbol but I can't find it anywhere. How can I get to it?

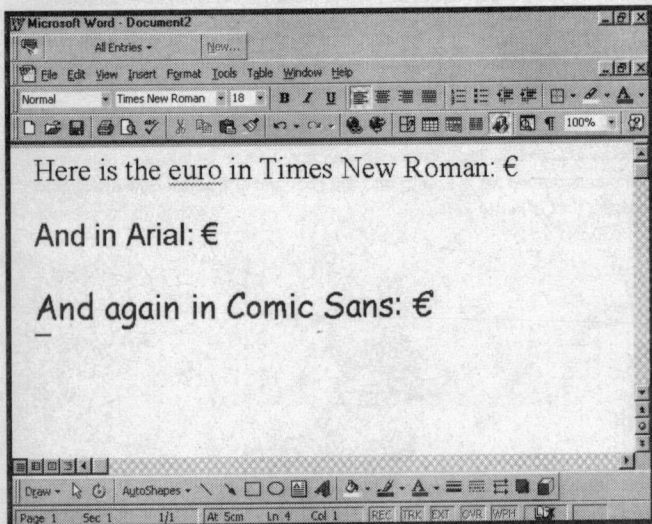

A I assume you have Windows 95, because 98 supports the Euro, as does NT 4 and the latest version of Windows CE. What you do is to go to that part of the Microsoft website which offers you a download of the Euro: www.microsoft.com/windows/euro.asp.

Follow the instructions, and when the program has loaded, go back to the start page and left click on the Microsoft typography link. There you will be told that you can access the symbol by clicking AltGr+4 (the normal 4, not the numeric keypad 4).

What doesn't appear to be documented is that you can also access the character by pressing Ctrl+Alt+4. Use the Character map to find out which fonts support the Euro: they are Arial, Comic Sans MS and Times New Roman. There's no hardship if the typeface you are using doesn't support the Euro. Simply swap faces for the symbol to Arial if you are using a sans serif face, otherwise use Times New Roman. If you use a lot of them, use a combination of characters you aren't using elsewhere in the text, eg EXXX.

Then, when you have finished working on the document, go for Alt+E, E to get up the Replace dialog box. At this point, you type EXXX or whatever in the first edit box, then Tab to the second box. Now click on the Format tab, and opt for Font.

Now you can change the font to, say, Comic Sans MS, and then type Ctrl+Alt+4 to get the Euro, and finally opt for Replace All. Alternatively, if you have the advanced knowledge, you could create a macro to do the job. More about this in a future question and answer session.

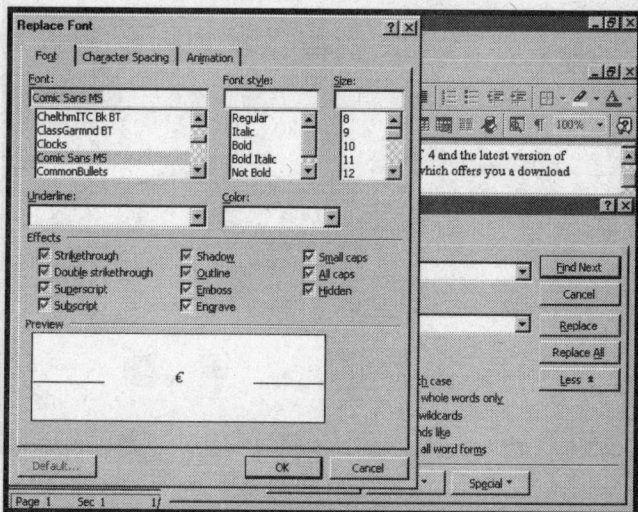

SPEEDING UP

Q I'm a complete beginner and I am just getting used to Windows. I understand there are ways of running programs more quickly than going to Start, Programs and so on. I like to use a graphics package, Microsoft Works and the built-in games a lot, as well as the Calculator and the Character Map. Can you tell me how I can speed things up, and which approach is best?

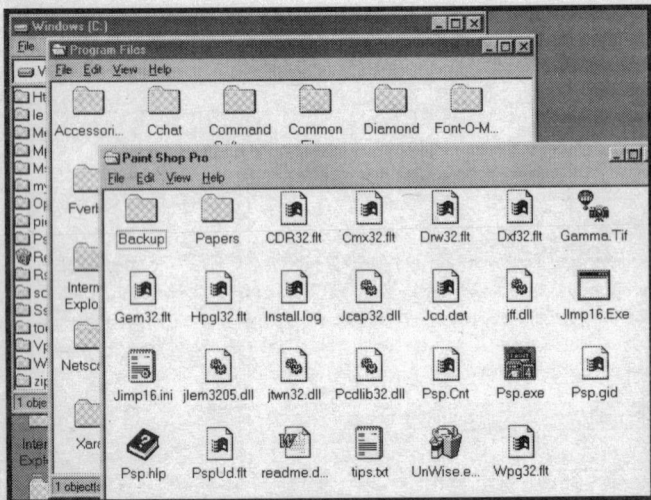

A To answer the last part of the question first: one of the neatest aspects of Windows for the user is that there are a variety of different ways of doing most things, and getting at your most frequently used programs is one case in point. There is no 'best' or 'right' way - it's up to you to choose what suits your needs, and how often and in what circumstances you use them. So, let me take you through the various approaches to speeding up the launching of applications, to use the technical term. The basic choices are: (a) putting an icon on the Desktop; (b) putting an icon on the Start menu; (c) automatically loading it when you start the computer and putting it on the Taskbar (Run Minimised).

Each has its pros and cons, and there is nothing to stop you from doing all three things to a particular application. Do note that the following instructions are not the only way of achieving your objectives, nor do they tell the whole story, but they do offer the simplest approach possible.

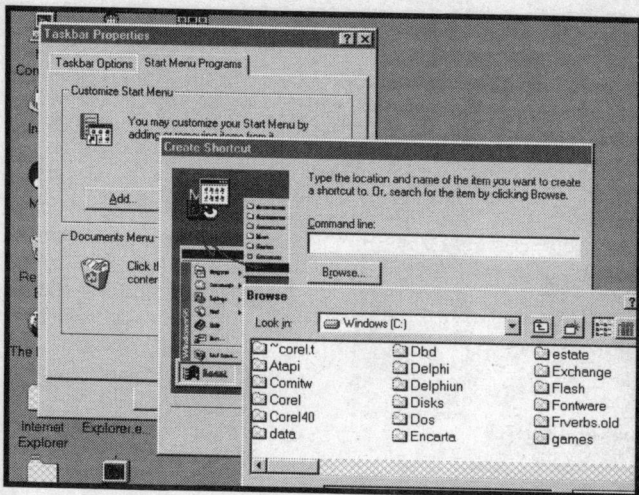

Taskbar Properties ? ×

Taskbar Options | Start Menu Programs

Customize Start Menu

You may customize your Start Menu by adding or removing items from it.

Add...

Documents Menu

Click t
conter

Create Shortcut

Type the location and name of the item you want to create a shortcut to. Or, search for the item by clicking Browse.

Command line:

Browse...

Browse ?

Look in: | Windows (C:)

~corel.t   Dbd   estate
Atapi   Delphi   Exchange
Comitw   Delphiun   Flash
Corel   Disks   Fontware
Corel40   Dos   Frverbs.old
data   Encarta   games

For options (a) and (b), clear the Desktop, then open My Computer. Open Program Files and you will see a number of folders, each of which represents an item on the Programs continuation menu. Open the folder you are inter-ested in and look for the EXE file for the application.

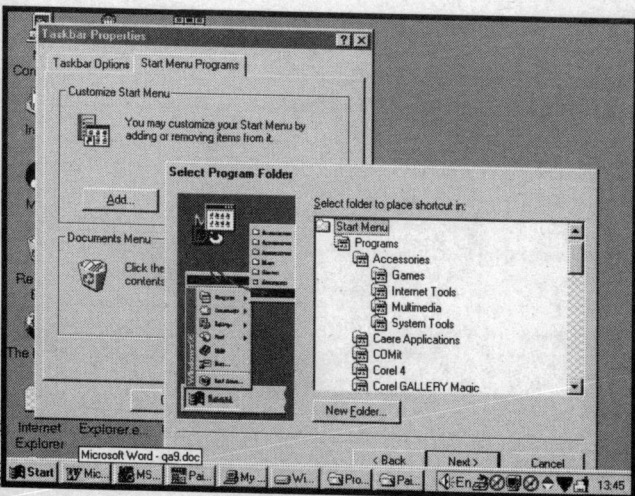

Taskbar Properties ? ×

Taskbar Options | Start Menu Programs

Customize Start Menu

You may customize your Start Menu by adding or removing items from it.

Add...

Documents Menu

Click the
contents

Select Program Folder

Select folder to place shortcut in:

Start Menu
  Programs
    Accessories
      Games
      Internet Tools
      Multimedia
      System Tools
    Caere Applications
    COMit
    Corel 4
    Corel GALLERY Magic

New Folder...

< Back   Next >   Cancel

Internet Explorer Explorer.e...

Microsoft Word - qa9.doc

Start | Mic... | MS... | Pai... | My... | Wi... | Pro... | Pai... | En... | 13:45

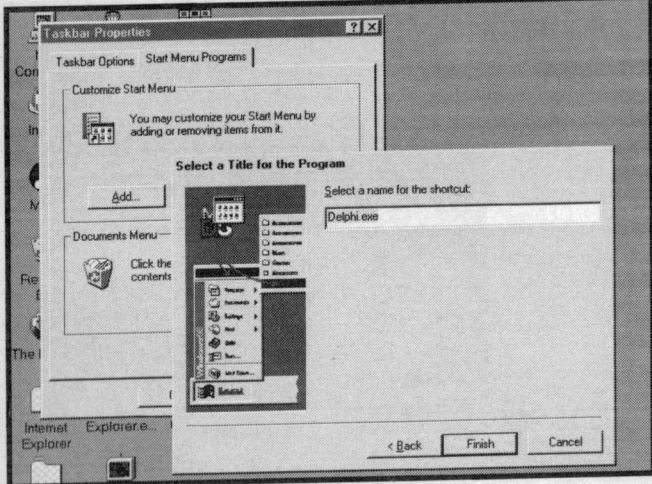

Hold down the right mouse button over the icon, drag it to the Desktop (by holding down the left button, moving the file and then releasing) and opt for 'Create Shortcut Here'. This will create an icon on the Desktop which, when you double left click on it, will launch the application.

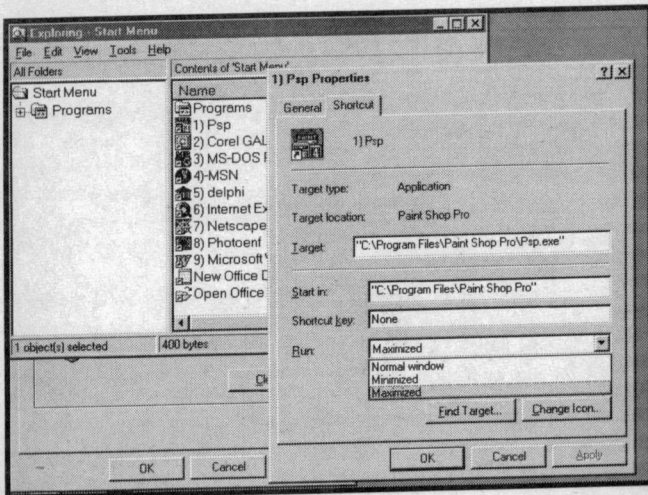

Shortcut to Psp.exe Properties ? X

General Shortcut

Shortcut to Psp.exe

Target type: Application

Target location: Paint Shop Pro

Target: "C:\Program Files\Paint Shop Pro\Psp.exe"

Start in: "C:\Program Files\Paint Shop Pro"

Shortcut key: F1

Provides a space for you to define a keyboard shortcut to start or switch to this program from Windows. Shortcut keys must include CTRL and/or ALT and another key; for example, CTRL +Y. You cannot use ESC, ENTER, TAB, SPACEBAR, PRINT SCREEN, or BACKSPACE.

No other program can use this key combination. If the shortcut key conflicts with an access key in a Windows program, the access key will not work.

Shortcut to Psp.exe

Explorer

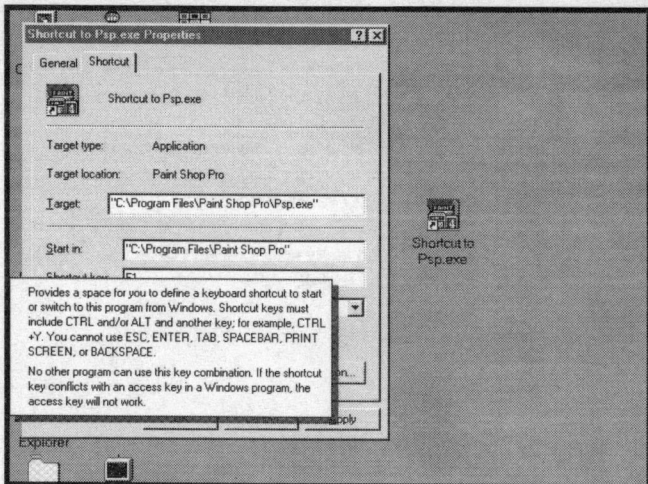

You can undo the action any time by right clicking on the icon and opting to delete it. Don't worry: deleting a short cut doesn't delete the application itself.

Alternatively, instead of dragging a copy of the EXE icon to the Desktop, you can drag it over the Start button, then let go. The icon then appears on the Start button and you just left click on it to launch the application.

More complicated is the situation which automatically runs the application when you switch on the computer, placing it on the Taskbar. Go for Start, Settings, Taskbar, and left click on the Start Menu Programs tab. Click Add, Browse and find your application, as you did above with My Computer. Double left click on the icon and you will see the full path to the program typed for you in the window. Look at the bottom of the dialog box, and you will see a button marked Next. Left click on that, and you will see one of those tree structures of folders. Double left click on the Start up folder and a window appears with the name of the program in it.

You can change that if you want to, but all you need now to do is to type Finish. To ensure that the program just ends up on the Taskbar (i.e. is run in minimised format), click on Advanced from the Taskbar Start Menu programs tab, right click on the icon of the program you want, go to Properties and then the Shortcut tab.

There is a drop-down menu for you to select whether the program is run in a normal window, maximised, or minimised. Make your choice, then close the dialog box. That should do the trick.

There is an additional approach which involves specifying a key combination as a shortcut. If you right click on a shortcut, go to Properties, then left click on the Shortcut tab. There is a box for you to specify a shortcut key, and it should currently state 'None'. Highlight the box.

At this point the fun starts. Even Help doesn't help much here, unless you press F1, at which point a hint box appears telling you what to do and to make matters worse, F1 appears in the box as the shortcut!

If you press, say, P, the shortcut comes up as Ctrl+Alt+P. All you then have to do is to remember the shortcut and make sure it doesn't clash with anything else. If you think it's all worthwhile, that is.

STUCK IN THE WEB

Q I'm not too clued up about websites, but I have managed to create my own home page. The trouble is that that when I change the name of the image it's often distorted. What am I doing wrong?

A A word of explanation first. You can easily put images on web pages using the <IMG> tag. Afterwards, IMG becomes the attribute SRC (source), with the path of the image file in double quotes. Then, you can specify a number of other attributes, including the height and width of the image.

As all these tags and their attributes are rather fiddly, it's more than tempting simply to copy and paste them in different parts of your code. However, the side effect of doing so, as you have discovered, is that if you have specified the height and width, you must change them to fit each image, otherwise you will get distortions.

If you believe that the best solution is not to specify the width and height at all, think again. Specifying both prevents the page being put on screen in a jerky fashion, with each image pushing the rest of the page sideways and downwards - not, you'll agree, very good for the presentation of your site.

In Paint Shop Pro you can go for File, Open, then just left click on the file you are interested in and the program will display the width and height in pixels, plus the colour depth. This information is also given for the currently selected open image on the status bar at the bottom of the screen.

NSF(S): Untitled - Netscape

File   Edit   View   Go   Window   Help

Distorting an image

Top   Home

Document: Done

UNDERSTANDING TABLES

Q I wanted to convert a booklist sent to me into a different format so I could load it into a spreadsheet. I thought I would convert tabs to commas but it wouldn't work. I attach a copy of the file. What can be done?

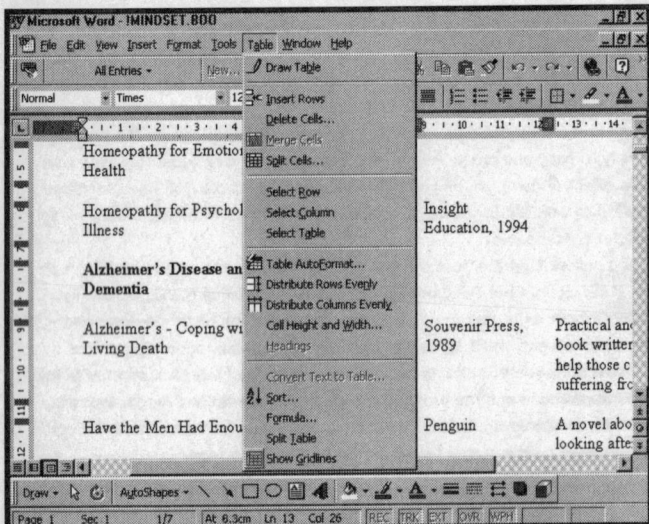

A This is one of those situations in which you can puzzle over the problem all day long and there seems to be no solution at all. For some reason, Word simply doesn't seem to want to play ball. The snag, though, is that your booklist isn't separated by tabs at all. It's in the form of a table and you need to convert the table to text before you can perform other operations on it.

Tables are often used to control the layout of your document, and they can be very elusive because there is no compulsion to put a border round a table or its individual components (or cells, as they are properly termed). The term 'table' is a little unfortunate, because it implies a classful of bored eight-year-olds merrily chanting 'Five tens are fifty' and so on, ad nauseam. In fact, tables don't have to have anything to do with numeric content at all.

You can put whatever you like in them. In fact, one of their main uses, particularly in website design, is to control the layout of the screen. HTML is

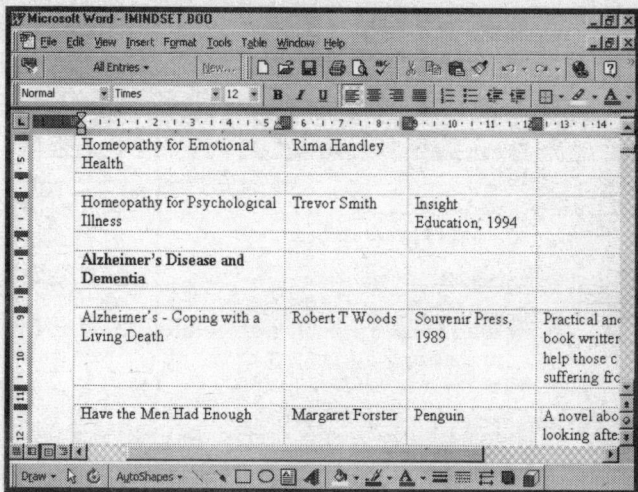

Homeopathy for Emotional Health	Rima Handley		
Homeopathy for Psychological Illness	Trevor Smith	Insight Education, 1994	
Alzheimer's Disease and Dementia			
Alzheimer's - Coping with a Living Death	Robert T Woods	Souvenir Press, 1989	Practical and book writter help those c suffering fro
Have the Men Had Enough	Margaret Forster	Penguin	A novel abo looking afte

designed to work with all kinds of screen sizes and resolutions, so it is important to ensure that, as far as possible, every end user gets the same output. Tables can be particularly useful when laying out images and text next to each other.

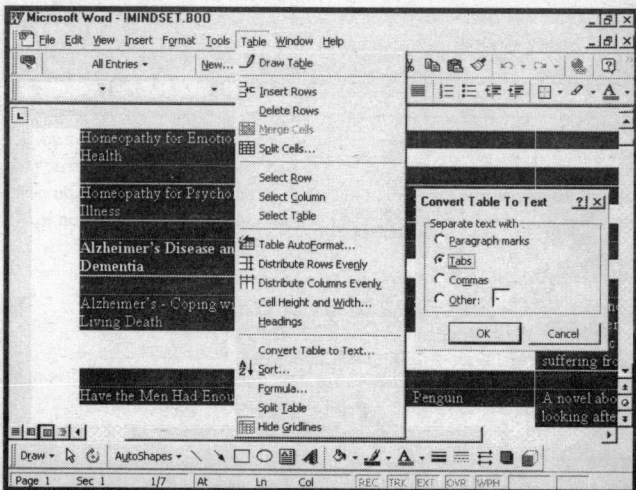

Microsoft Works

File Edit View Insert Format Tools Window Help

Arial   ▼ 10 ▼

A1   "Alternative Medicine

Sheet1

BIT.TXT

	A	B	C	D	E	F	G	H
1	Alternative Medicine							
2								
3	Homeopath	Rima Handley						
4								
5	Homeopath	Trevor Smith	Insight Educ	1994				
6								
7	Alzheimer's Disease and Dementia							
8								
9	Alzheimer's	Robert T W	Souvenir Pri	1989	Practical and			
10	sympathetic book written especially to help those caring for someone suffering from dementia.							
11								
12	Have the M	Margaret Fc	Penguin	A novel about a family looking after a				
13	grandmother with dementia.							
14								
15	Dementia: Money and L	Alzheimer SA useful and clearly						
16	written guide with dementia sufferers in mind but of interest to anyone involved in helping a per							
17	who is finding it difficult to manage their money or personal affairs.							

You can tell if you are dealing with a table either from the presence of table
cell markers on the rulers, or you can opt for Table, Show Gridlines - and the
lines round the table cells will then appear. The question now is how to convert the table to text form.

National Schizophrenia Fellowship (Scotland) - Netscape

File Edit View Go Window Help

Back Forward Reload Home Search Guide Print Security Stop

Bookmarks Location: file:///cl/nsf/text/who.htm

Chairman

Chairman:
Fred Bloggins

Chief Executive Officer

CEO:
Joe Smith

Document Done

Left click anywhere on the table, then press Alt+5, the 5 being on the numeric pad, but with the Num Lock key switched off (sorry about the complications, but that's what the system requires). Now left click the Convert Table to Text option on the Table menu and up pops a little dialog box which asks how you would like the individual cells to be separated. For information on converting just part of a table, go to Help, 'tables, converting text and tables'.

As I said earlier, tables are used on the Internet to control the layout of the page. You can also use the borders attribute to create special effects, especially if you set the border to something like 10. That generates a wide frame round an image.

BAD LANGUAGE

Q I am using MS Office 97: Professional Edition. Following the instructions in the magazine, I have attempted to change the language on Word from American English to British English, under Tools, Language. All appears to be well, but the next time I started the computer, it reverted to US English. What can I do to make it permanent, and also to stop those annoying red lines under words which are correctly spelled in British English, like 'colour' for 'color'?

A You should recognise that there is a difference between changing something which is local to your application and the overriding settings of the computer as a whole. In other words, your machine is set up with American English as the default, and what you are doing is simply altering that default during the time at which Word is running.

The way of overcoming the problem is to change the machine settings themselves. The way to do that is to go to Start, Settings, Control Panel, Keyboard. If you look at the information on the Language tab, you will see that your default language is American English.

The reason why the spell check doesn't like 'colour' is that it is working from American English, so all should now be well.

CONTROLLING HEADERS

Q I have a problem with headers. I designed a nice piece of headed paper using the header (seemed pretty appropriate to me), but it will insist on appearing at the top of every page in the letter. Help!

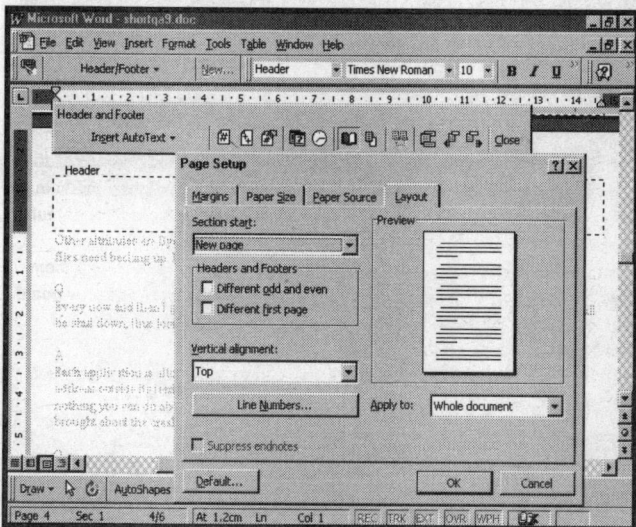

A The answer to your question is to go to View, Header and Footer and left click on the sixth item on the toolbar, Page Setup. Then you can specify a different header/footer for the first page, as well as for odd and even pages.

A brief reminder for those not familiar with these options: It's quite common to have a different header and footer on the title page of a document. For example, you may well not want to have the page number appear, or the running head which you may use in the rest of the document.

The 'running head' has nothing to do with a bad cold. It's the text you put along the top of the page as the title of the document or chapter. You may want to put the title on the left-hand page and the name of the author on the right. At the foot of the page, you may want the page number out to the left on the left-hand page, and out to the right on a right-hand page.

Do remember that the header and footer typeface and point size need to match that of the text of your document, and with a bit of thought you can come up with some very interesting effects. For example, you can create a text box taking up the space occupied by the header, set the Fill colour (on the Drawing toolbar) to grey, the text to white, and then experiment with different fonts and sizes.

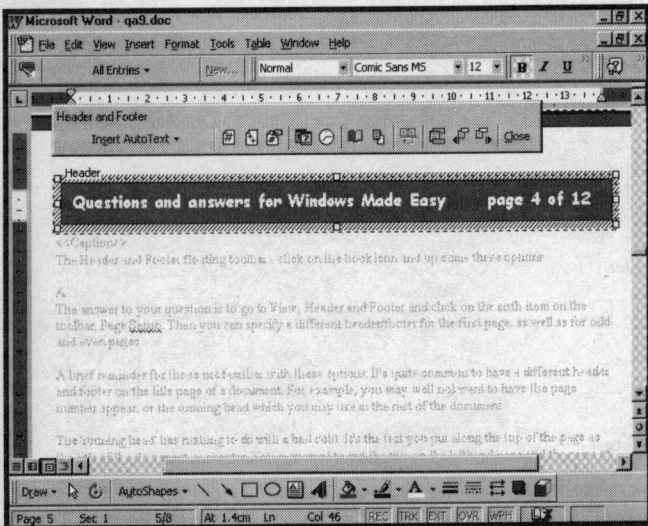

ONE FONT ONLY

Q How can I install a single font from my Corel Draw CD-ROM without having to install all of them, wasting precious disk space?

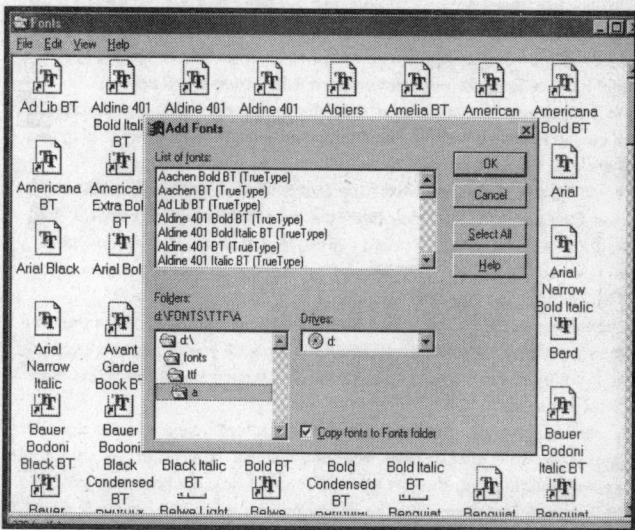

A Sounds simple, but actually there's more than meets the eye to this question. Assumption number one is that you have to use Corel Draw's facilities for installing fonts, and number two is that they take up a lot of space. There's an additional twist, which relates to a question from another reader who found the folder Windows\ Fonts, copied a font file to it and wonders why he can't access it.

Let's start with the last issue. You can put a font file anywhere you like on your system, but it won't recognise it until you have gone through a process called 'installation', which means telling the computer that there is a font around called Fred or Joe and where it is. We'll look at that in detail in a moment or two.

The second issue relates to space. A font file can take up to 80,000 bytes or more, but if you install a font, it can be installed by reference to its location on the CD-ROM. You don't have to copy the file to the hard drive. However, there is a catch to this. If you have a number of fonts scattered across various CD-ROMs, you either have to be pretty nimble swapping them in and out of the drives, or you can't use them, which causes odd problems with the computer, particularly if you have a helpful setup which tries to find a similar font to the one you ask for. Sometimes, the definition of 'similar' is a touch bizarre.

So, to the first question: how to go about installing one font by leaving it in place on the CD-ROM. Say you want to install the font called Benguiat from your Corel Draw CD-ROM (it will be different on other programs, but you should be able to figure out what's where without too much bother).

Go to Settings on the Start menu, then opt for Control Panel and double left click on the Fonts icon. Up comes the contents of the Windows/Fonts folder. Left click on File on the main menu, and then on Install new fonts.

Now you have to winkle out where the font is located on the CD-ROM, so change the Drive to D, and look down the list of folders which pops up. You should find a folder helpfully called Fonts. Open that up, and you see three more folders. Opt for the TTF folder. TTF stands for True Type Font, meaning one which looks the same on the screen as it does on the printer.

The computer spends a few moments retrieving file names (more of that in a moment), then all you do is scroll down the list until you find the font you are after. If you have the Copy fonts to font folder box checked, the actual file will get copied across.

Now just load an application and check that the font appears in the alphabetical list. If you want to copy fonts from one machine to another, you may come up against a little snag, the one I hinted at when talking about 'retrieving file names'. Not all fonts are called by an obvious name. In fact, Benguiat Bold BT has the tongue-twisting title TT0127M_.TTF. So, you have to go to the fonts folder, find the font you are after, right click on it and take a note of what its real name is.

Then you can copy it and install it elsewhere, copyright requirements permitting. If you want to try before you buy, so to speak, open the folder you want using My Computer, then right click on the font of your choice (again you may come up against the odd filenames which many fonts have), left click Open, and you'll see a demo of the font.

WEBPAGE THUMBNAILS

Q One of the commonly used techniques on the web is for people to present you with a number of thumbnails, from which you choose which images to enlarge by clicking on them. My question is: Do you have to have a separate file for the thumbnails, or can you just have one image, squeezed down to a small size for the thumbnail and left as it is for the full-sized picture?

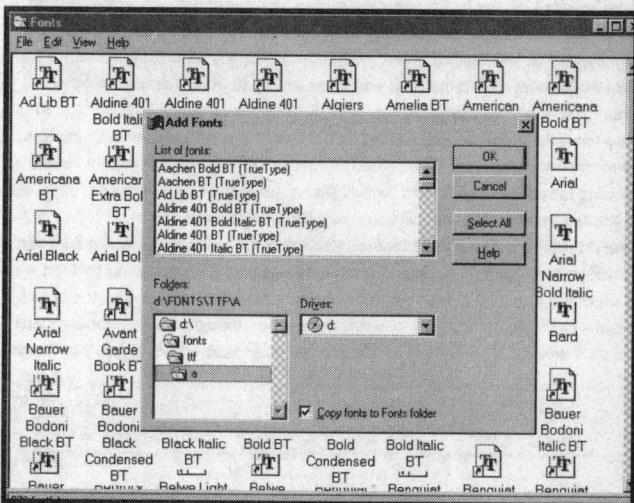

A The background to this question is that you can specify what size your image is reproduced in. So, if you have a whopping great image 1000 bytes by 1000 bytes, you could show it as a thumbnail of 100 x 100 by specifying the width and height of the image.

But don't do this. Avoid using a large image because the whole point of thumbnails is that they are quicker to load than the full size image - so, even if they are squeezed down, the full image takes just as long to load, and which, if squashed up, may well look rather odd.

One piece of advice: Do make your thumbnails large enough for the user to get an idea of what their content is (100 x 100 pixels is pretty OK). As an aid to this, don't forget the Alt attribute, which allows you to put a written description of the image in double quotes, and this appears if the mouse pointer moves over the thumbnail.

THE FLOATING TOOLBAR

Q I changed screen resolution so that I could do screen dumps in a fixed 640x480 format. Unfortunately, the toolbar in Word disappeared off the right-hand side of the screen and I wasn't able to change the box which specified the size of the text on the screen (100 per cent, or greater or smaller). How can I get at stuff that has disappeared off the end of the screen like that?

A If you look at the Toolbars option on the View menu you will probably find that you have three or four items ticked. That means the rest are currently not available to you. Spend a few moments finding out what they are and if you might need them. The toolbars themselves are by default 'docked'; in other words, they are fixed along the top or bottom of the screen.

If you examine them closely, you will see a raised double vertical line, which is called the 'move handle'. If you place the mouse pointer over it, hold it down and drag it over the document, it changes shape to a normal-looking outline rectangle. Release the button and you now have a floating toolbar.

If you do this to the Standard toolbar, you'll find the percentage size drop-down list sitting there waiting for you to use. To turn it back into a docked toolbar, hold the mouse pointer down on the title bar and drag it back to the top of the screen - or the bottom, if you so wish. Remember, though, floating toolbars can be a mixed blessing. Murphy's Law seems to state that wherever you put them,

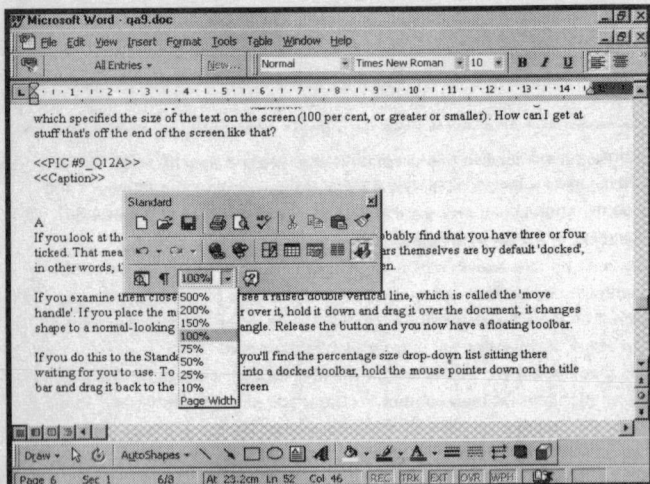

A NASTY TURN

Q I can't find a way in Paint Shop 4.12 to rotate text. There used to be a command to put it on the screen on its side. What do I do?

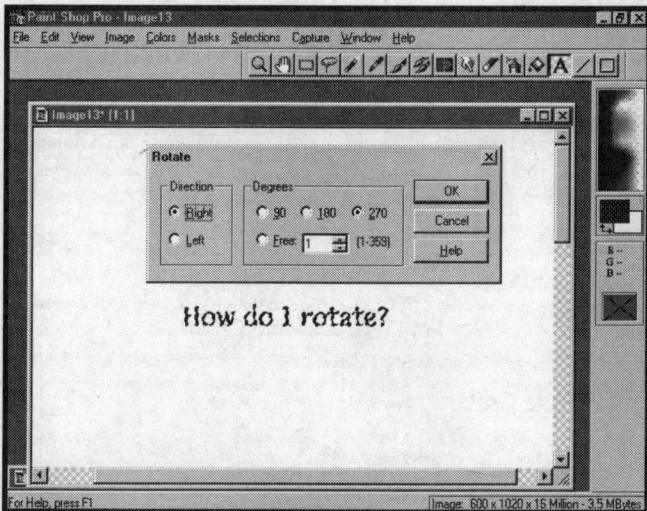

A You are missing a key feature of Paint Shop, and that is that when you select part of an image or have text on the screen with wobbly lines round (meaning you can edit it), commands refer not to the whole image but just to the selected bit. So you can rotate text by placing it on the image and before it's fixed - in other words, when it still has a moving dotted line round it - opt for Image, Rotate and move it the amount you want.

The same can be done with a selected part of the image, using either the rectangular or freelance selection tools.

A CASE OF CAPS

Q I tend to be a bit clumsy with the keyboard, but I really did something daft the other day. Somehow or other, the whole memo came out as capital letters. I tried the trick I read about in Windows Made Easy whereby you press Shift+F3 to switch from caps to initial caps and to lower case, but that didn't work. I had to start all over again. What did I do - and how can I stop it happening again?

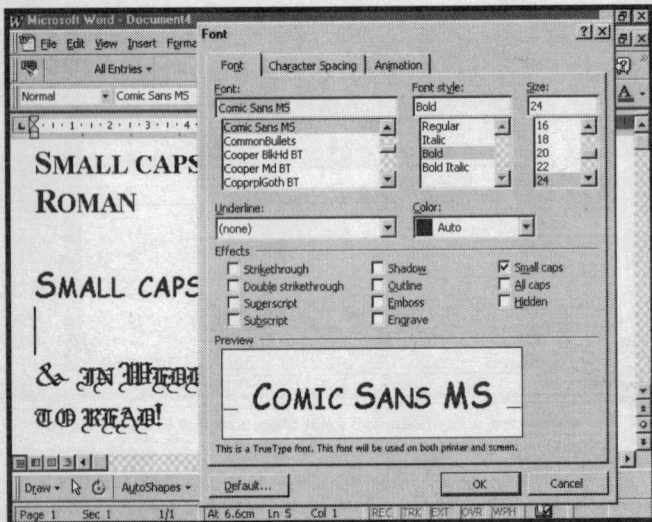

A You wouldn't like to send easier questions in by any chance, would you? What finally gave the game away was the copy of the memo which you sent in with your letter. It's nothing to do with the Caps Lock refusing to switch itself off as you suggested.

The beginning of the memo gives your initials - OFM - and what appears to have happened, by a freak of Murphy's Law, is that you must have quickly typed OFM with your finger on the Alt key instead of the Shift key.

You probably didn't realise you had done this and retyped the name, but then found the rest of the memo came out, not in caps as you state, but in small caps for the letters you wanted as lower case. The reason? If you press Alt+O you get to the Format menu, F gets you to the Font option, and the key combination Alt+M puts a tick in the small caps check box.

SMALL CAPS IN USE IN TIMES NEW ROMAN

SMALL CAPS IN COMIC SANS MS

& IN WEDDING TEXT – NOT SO EASY TO READ!

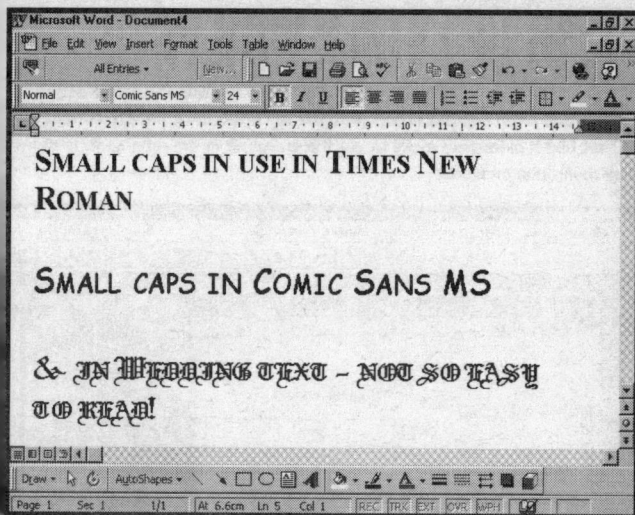

Incidentally, you don't have to press Alt+F to get to the Font option, but the system doesn't seem to mind whether you type plain F or Alt+F. Change the name of your company - or type a bit more carefully in future.

A SPOT OF BOTHER WITH PAINT

Q I'm having trouble with Paint Shop Pro. I use the rectangular selection tool and often want to select from the top left-hand corner (co-ordinate 0,0), but find it extremely tricky to get the crosshair in the right spot. Is there a way round this problem?

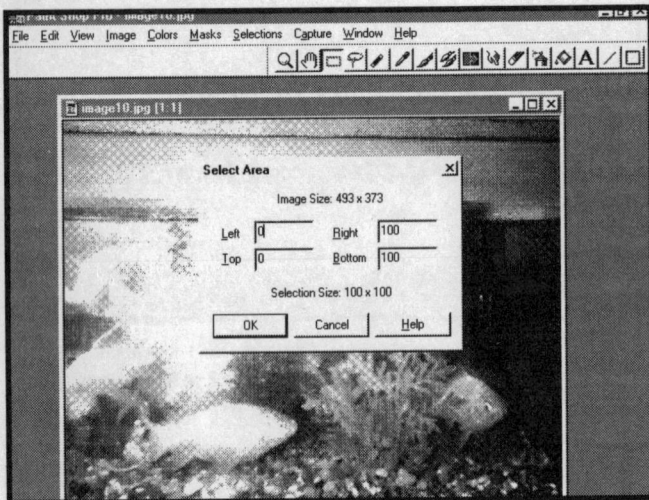

A What you are referring to is the fact that, when you move the crosshair into the top left-hand corner, you probably find it will go to 0,1 or 1,0 but then falls off the edge of the image, so to speak, and disappears. That can be a trifle annoying.

Two points: If you are wanting to copy the entire image to the Clipboard, left click on the top bar and then press Alt+E, C. If you know the co-ordinates you are after for the part of the image you want, double left click on the dotted rectangular toolbar item and up will come a dialog box which allows you to specify the co-ordinates by number. You could, of course, also use MouseKeys to move the mouse pointer around in accurate steps.

For information on MouseKeys, go to Help, MouseKeys. It's part of the Accessibilites option for those who have difficulties using the computer, but there is no reason why you should not exploit it.

A BAD START

Q When I want to insert an image into Word, the program always starts at the Clipart folder. What a nuisance - I want it to start somewhere else, and I have to painstakingly find my way there before I can get to work. Can I improve things?

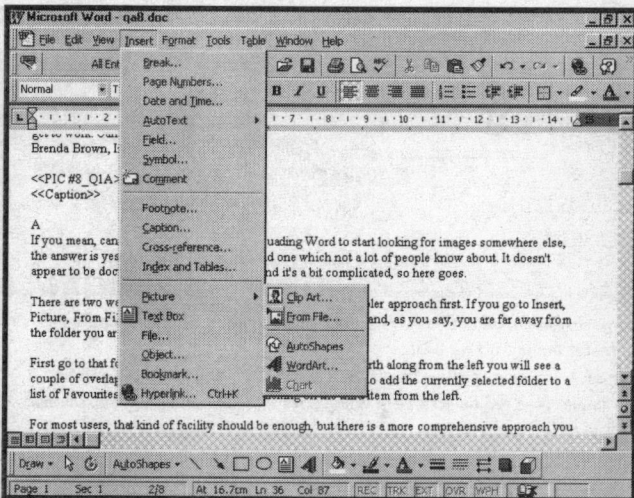

A If you mean, can you improve things by persuading Word to start looking for images somewhere else, the answer is yes. It's a very powerful tool and one which not a lot of people know about. It doesn't appear to be documented in the online help and it's a bit complicated, so here goes. There are two ways of resolving the problem. Let's take the simpler approach first. If you go to Insert, Picture, From File you end up with a pretty daunting dialog box and, as you say, you are miles away from the folder you are after.

First make your way to the folder you want, then look at the items on the Toolbar. Fourth along from the left you will see one with a couple of overlapping folders and a plus sign. This is the option which allows you to add the currently selected folder to a list of Favourites, which you can access by clicking on the third item from the left, the Look in Favourites icon.

That makes the game of Hunt The Folder a lot easier. For most users, that kind of facility should be enough, but there is a more comprehensive

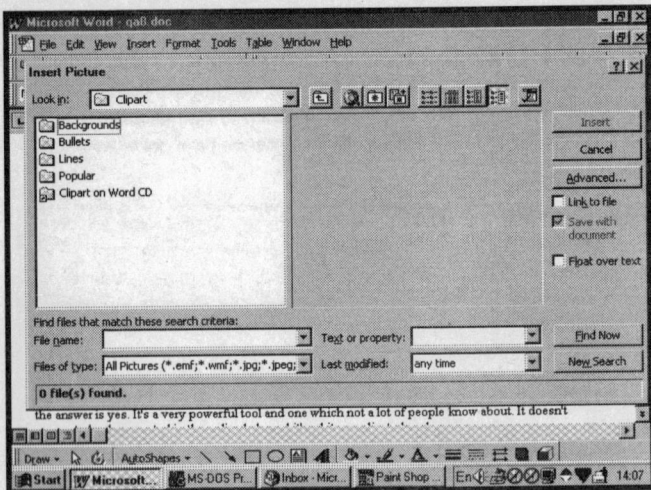

approach you can adopt. From the dialog box, identify the Advanced button on the Insert Picture dialog box.

Click on Advanced, then on the arrow against the 'Look in' drop-down list. If your image files are on your hard drive, opt for C: and press Cancel. Choose

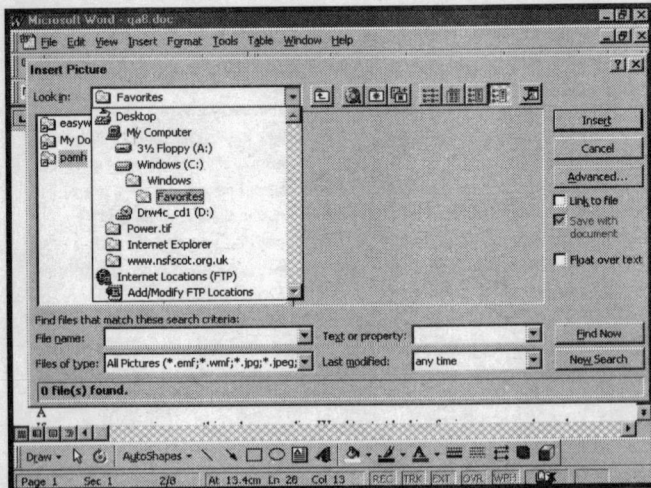

the first folder you want to add to your list, then click on Advanced again. This time, you will see the full path name of the folder in the 'Look in' edit box. Locate the 'Save Search' button and click on it. Up comes a window with an edit box called 'Name for this Search'. Choose an appropriate name - like 'Christmas graphics', 'Family images', 'Business logos', or whatever - and type it in.

Repeat the process until the list of items is complete. Now when you want to search in one of those folders, go to Insert, Picture, From Folder, and then on to Advanced. Press Open Search, select the name you want from the list and click on Find Now. It takes a bit longer than the Favourites method, but it gets you to any one of a long list of folders of your choice by descriptive name, and will help you if you have a large number of images in different categories, with each set in a folder of their own.

TAKE NOTE

Q I can't get the hang of Notepad. I was given a text file to edit and I put it in a particular folder, but when I look there it isn't there, if you see what I mean. I am a real beginner, but can you help?

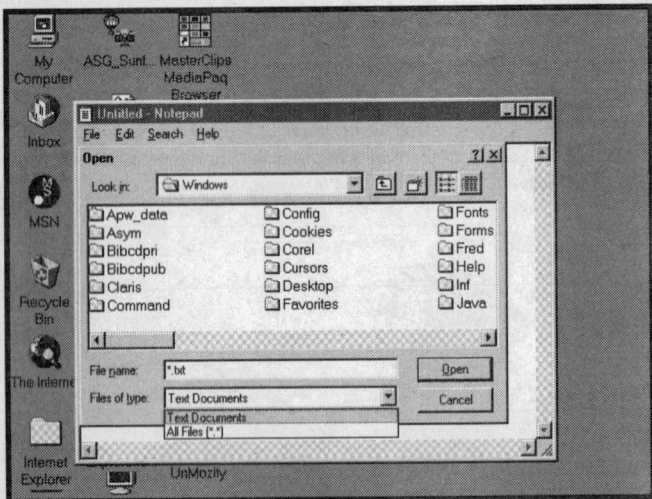

A What has probably happened is that the file you were given didn't have the extension TXT. When Notepad looks in a folder for files, it is by default looking only for those with a TXT extension. To change that, you have to click on the downwards pointing arrow to produce the drop-down list with the alternative All Files option.

It is important to familiarise yourself with the common extensions so that you know what means what. The easiest way to do this is to open My Computer, then click on View, Options. Click on the File Types tab and then scroll down the list, highlighting the items. You will see that there is a huge number of registered file extension names.

The ones you are most likely to come across are: EXE (an application), DOC (a Word document), WBK (Word backup file), and TXT (Notepad file), but I leave you to look down the list as there are lots more.

PRINTER PROBLEMS

Q In the old mainframe days, lineprinter paper (by which I mean the fan-fold continuous stationery) had a header page for each separate bit of output, so that the user could be identified and the operator could separate the output more easily. We have a high volume printer on our network. Is it possible to have a similar page under Windows using Word 97?

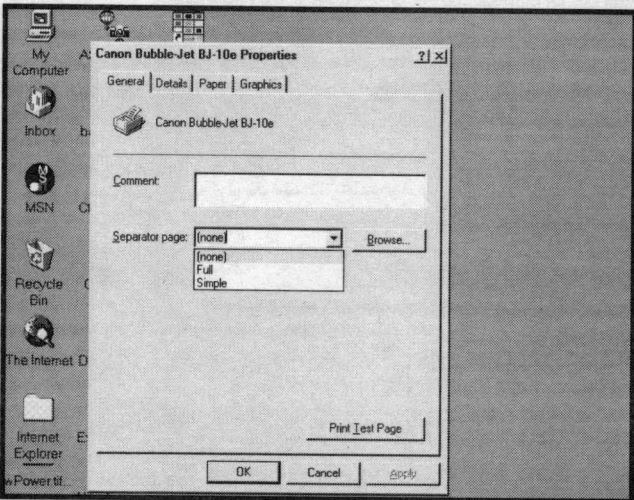

A If the printer is directly attached to your computer, open the Printers folder. This can be done either from the Control Panel or from Printer on the Settings option on the Start menu. First, click on a printer to select it. Then, on the File menu, you will find a Properties option. Go for that option, then click on the General tab. One of the choices you will find there is that of a Separator Page. Choose the one you want, or browse for a custom page you designed.

Although you can only set up separator pages when your printer is directly connected, there is nothing to stop you from inserting a separator page of your own at the beginning of each document. At this point, you may object that this puts your page numbering out of joint. Not a bit - providing you go to View, Header and Footer, click on Format Page Number, and in the edit box marked Start at, put a zero.

MY MUDDY HOME PAGE

Q I hope this isn't too obscure a question, but I have been tinkering around with designing a home page for myself on the Internet. I found out somewhere that you can specify not only the background colour, but also a pattern using an image. So I created what I thought was a nice pale blue pattern with the words My Home Page repeated across and down the page. However, it came out all horrible and muddy grey. What did I do wrong?

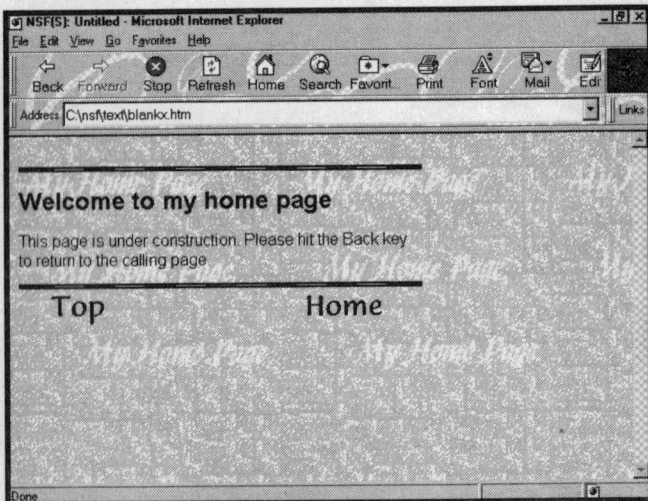

A Near the beginning of your HTML file, there is a tag called BODY, and, as you say, you can specify the background colour (note the American spelling BGCOLOR), either as a word in quotes, like "blue" or "green", or as a hexadecimal value in quotes, such as "#FFFFFF", for example, which in this case turns red, green and blue on full to create white.

We shall return to this feature in a moment. You can also specify - either instead of, or as well as, BGCOLOR - an image which acts as a wallpaper to your page. There are two important design points to note. The first is that the image repeats itself like Windows wallpaper can, and it should be created in such a way that the join between copies doesn't show.

To some extent this is a matter of trial and error. If you have come across sites with coloured or patterned backgrounds with unsightly lines on them, it's because the designer hasn't been careful enough in creating the background pattern.

The second design point is that the whole purpose of a Web site is to convey information, and if your background patter is too cluttered and isn't matched by foreground text in the appropriate colour, it will be hard to read, and potential visitors will be turned off.

Now to your specific problem: the clue to the image having a muddy appearance lies in the fact that, by default, the background colour of a Web page is grey, presumably the button grey of Windows.

You might well think that your image covers that default background, but what has happened is that you have created a GIF image with the trans-

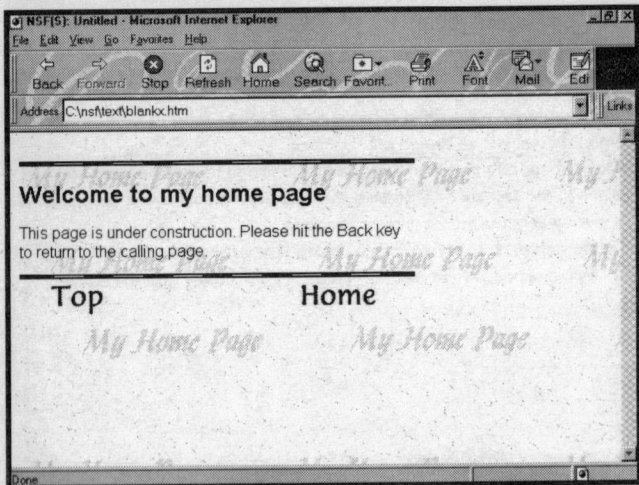

```
NSF(5): Untitled - Microsoft Internet Explorer
File Edit View Go Favorites Help

Back  Forward  Stop  Refresh  Home  Search  Favorit.  Print  Font  Mail  Edit

Address C:\nsf\text\blankx.htm                                    Links
```

Welcome to my home page

This page is under construction. Please hit the Back key
to return to the calling page.

Top   Home

parency value set to the background colour of that image. In other words, the
GIF image is "see through", and it will allow the background colour of the Web
page to show.

That is why you have a muddy image, with those bits of your GIF image which
are in the background colour turning a dull grey. Having nailed the problem,
the next question is what to do about it.

There are two ways of tackling the problem. Either process the image so that
it doesn't contain any background transparency information or, more easily
perhaps, set the background colour of the Web page to whatever you want it
to be, which brings us neatly back to BGCOLOR.

So if you wanted your background colour to be white and your image is called
MYIMAGE, your code would go like this:

```
<BODY BGCOLOR="#FFFFFF" BACKGROUND="../image/myimage.gif">
```

At this point you can also specify the text colour using TEXT, again with a hex
value in double quotes or one of the standard colours as names, also in double quotes.

172

INDENT RULES

Q I can't get the hang of indenting in Word. Can you help me out?

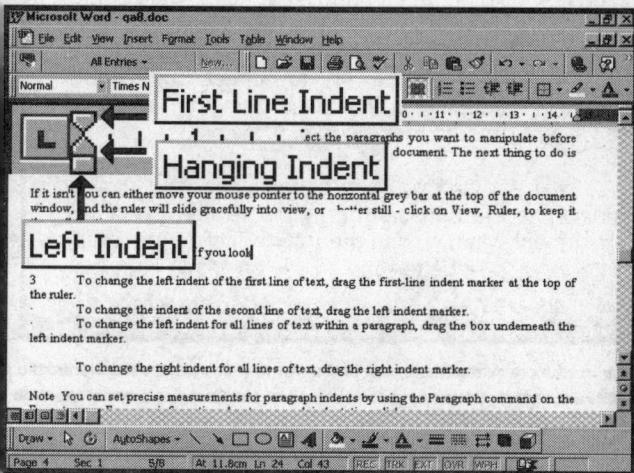

A The first point to remember is that you should select the paragraphs you want to manipulate before doing anything else, or use Alt+E and Select All to affect the whole document. The next thing to do is to ensure that the ruler is visible.

If it isn't, you can either move your mouse pointer to the horizontal grey bar at the top of the document window, and the ruler will slide gracefully into view, or - better still - click on View, Ruler, to keep it there all the time.

The three markers on the ruler have the following functions, starting at the top: left indent, hanging indent and first line indent. Place the mouse pointer over the one you wish to move, then shift it to the right. You'll see a dotted line down the screen showing you the effect of your action and, when you release the mouse, the change will take place. Remember the editor's friend, Ctrl+Z, to undo any action you don't like.

The first line indent marker indents the first line in the paragraph. The left indent marker indents all the lines in the paragraph. Finally, the hanging indent, which sounds a bit ominous, 'hangs' the second and subsequent lines of a paragraph below one another rather than at the left-hand margin. Try out the various options and see what the results are.

The first point to remember is that you should select the paragraphs you want to manipulate before doing anything else, or use Alt+E and Select All to affect the whole document. The next thing to do is to ensure that the ruler is visible.

If it isn't you can either move your mouse pointer to the horizontal grey bar at the top of the document window, and the ruler will slide gracefully into view, or - better still - click on View, Ruler, to

If you need more advanced control of the way in which paragraphs are indented in different styles, your starting point should be the Paragraph menu option on the Format menu. Here you can specify exact positionings for different styles in your text. For more detailed information, check out Outline View in Word Help.

HAVING A QUICK PEEK

Q Is there any way of using Quick View to look at HTML source files, rather than the actual Web page?

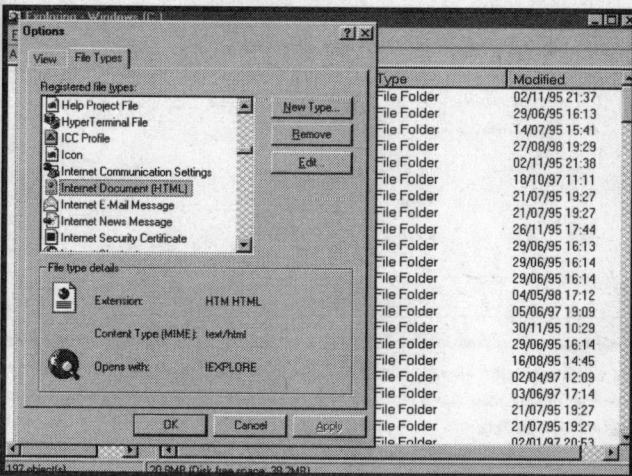

A A brief word of explanation first for those of you unfamiliar with how Web pages work. The HTML (HyperText Markup Language) files contain the information which allows the browser to set out a web page in all its glory, and these are plain text files, so they can be read by anyone. Anyone interested in seeing how Web pages work can see the underlying code by opting for View, Source (Internet Explorer) or View, Page Source (Netscape Navigator).

The benefit of Internet Explorer is that you can actually edit the source (it's in a Notepad file), and if you have the material off-line, it's a good way of tinkering with pages or developing web pages of your own. It's real-time computing, in the sense that, as soon as you hit Alt+F, S to save the HTML file, you can see the results for yourself by reloading the page.

A word of warning: If you are using frames, Internet Explorer gives you the HTML code which sets up the frames, rather than the visible pages, and when it refreshes, it goes back to that page rather than the subpage you are on. The way round this is to load just the page you want to work on. Remember, too, that you can have more than one version of Notepad running at any one time.

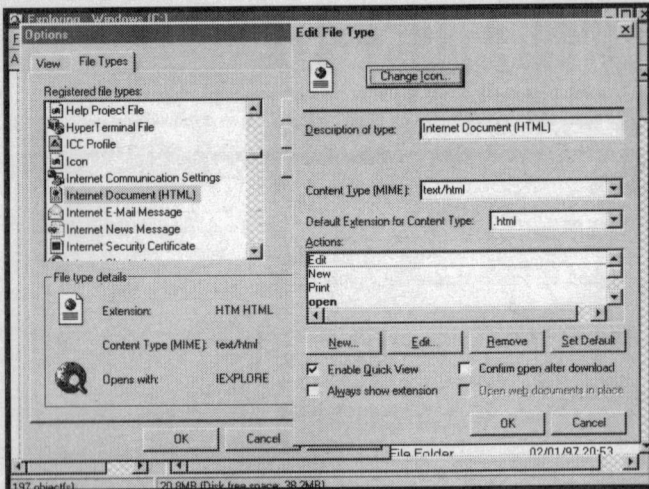

Now to the question about Quick View to inspect the code. There is indeed a way of achieving this. Open Explorer and then go for View, Options and click on the File Type Tab.

Scroll the window down until you get to the item called Internet Document (or

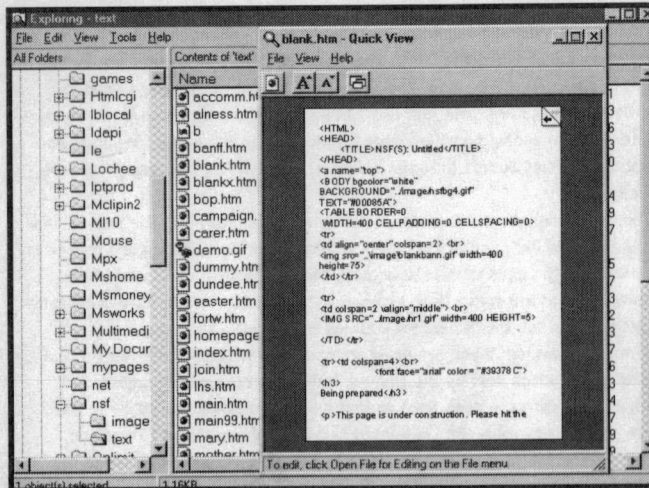

some similar wording). Click on that to highlight it, then click on the Edit button. At this point, you should see a check box called Enable Quick View. Check it. Now try it out by going to a folder in which you have HTML files, and right click on a file. Go for View and you will see the source code. Keep clicking on the box with the large A to increase the size of the text and the small A to reduce it. Click on the arrows on the paper fold at the top right-hand corner to move through the document.

That's all fine if you just want to look at the source code, but if you intend to edit it, either use Notepad or the more powerful MS-DOS Edit program. With Notepad, remember than when you try and open an HTML file you have to opt to view all files, otherwise it will only show TXT files.

Edit allows search and replace and you can have multiple files on the go at the same time, but it doesn't have the option to word wrap which Notepad has. To emulate multiple file editing with Notepad, keep opening a new instance of Notepad, but do avoid the pitfall of having the same file open in two different windows. Confusion may result, to put it mildly.

HOW MUCH SPACE?

Q Without having to use my fingers or a calculator, how can I find out how much space is taken up by a folder and the folders beneath it?

A Let's assume you have a folder called Winword and under it all the separate subfolders for different kinds of document.

Right click on Winword and choose Properties. You can see the number of folders and files and the size of the whole lot. You can access this option from any situation in which you have a folder on screen, whether it be on the Desktop, in Explorer, My Computer, or from typing START plus a folder name in the MS-DOS Window.

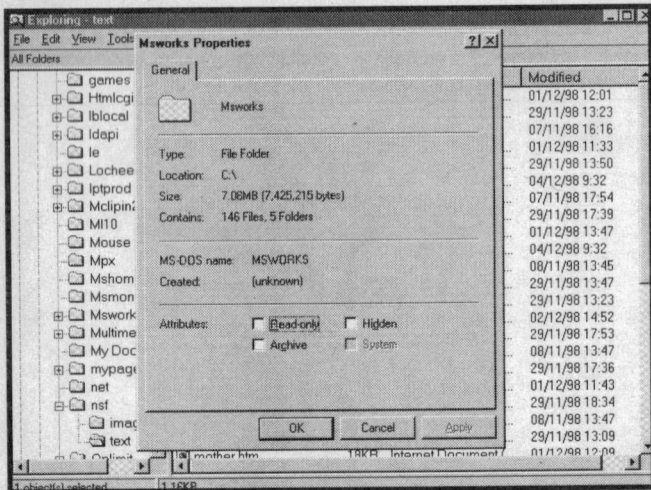

WHICH RESOLUTION?

Q I have designed a Web page using two frames, one on the left to allow the user to click on items to navigate round the site, while the rest of the screen is for the pages themselves. I designed this on a 17 inch screen with 1024 x 768 resolution and was frightfully proud of what I had done. Imagine my dismay when I looked at it on a friend's screen with a resolution of 640 x 480.

There was a slide bar to the right of the menu and that meant the left-hand side of the main page was squashed right up against the slide bar, not looking quite as elegant as I hoped. What can I do?

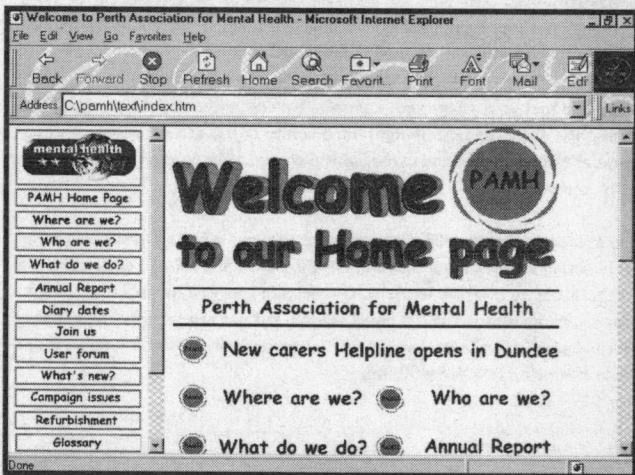

A Getting layouts right in all conditions is one of the real problems of Web page design. The idea is that you should be able to load Web pages on any computer (or platform, to use the technical term), but the disadvantage to that is that screen sizes vary. A standard screen is 640 x 480 resolution, but a notepad for example will probably be 800 x 600, and I understand that the screen resolution of any interactive digital TV Web surfing will be quite a bit smaller than that.

Not only do you have to cope with different sizes of resolution, but also there are different browsers for presenting Web pages. They boil down to Internet Explorer and Netscape Navigator as the two main players, and it isn't unreasonable to assume that people should have version 3 or above of either of them.

You should add a line of code to your loading page if you are using frames to point people in the direction of a Web site where they can download a newer version. This is done with the NO FRAMES command.

Further complications arise, especially with more advanced Web programming, where VBScript and JavaScript jostle for supremacy. Confusingly, Explorer uses both, but Navigator uses only JavaScript at the time of writing.

That is a quick tour of the Web programming minefield, so back to your specific problem. What clearly happened is that with a high screen resolution, all your left-hand side menu fitted on to a single screen, so there were no scrollbars, but on a lower resolution, it fell off the bottom of the screen and so Windows provided scrollbars You can switch them off with SCROLLING="no", but there's not much point doing that unless it's just a decorative frame without the information the user needs to access.

If you are working on a high resolution screen, the moral of the story is that you should test your pages with a smaller window, either by reducing the size of the page using the bottom right-hand corner of the screen or the centre button at the top right-hand corner of the screen. Alternatively, if you have the ability to change the screen resolution on the fly, do so.

Now, at last, to the specific problem which sparked off this answer. The solution is actually very straightforward. For the right-hand FRAME command, just add the attribute MARGIN WIDTH=10 which will give you enough of a margin to let it look uncrowded with a small screen, but not too far apart from the left-hand side with a larger resolution. For horizontally oriented frames, there is also a MARGIN HEIGHT attribute.

DOS TAKE-OVER

Q When I turn on my PC after showing the Windows 95 Intro screen it drops into the MS-DOS screen. Then when I type WIN to get Windows, it tells me I am already running Windows. I have recently been trying to load a DOS game, called Theme Park. What can I do?

A It looks as if Theme Park has grabbed hold of the system and autoloaded when you switch on. It seems to be running in a DOS full screen window in Windows, if you see what I mean. To close the window, type EXIT. You should scan the instructions for the game carefully, as it ought not to take over the system in such a way.

DEFAULT FONT BLUES

Q Every time I load Word or any of its variants (using Works, for example, or WordPad), it comes up with Times New Roman 10 point. I do not like Times New Roman, and especially not at that midget size. I much prefer Arial 11 point as my standard typeface, so this is irritating, especially as the default always seems to be lurking in the background ready to trip you up when, for example, you go to the end of a document and start typing there. Can you change the default typeface?

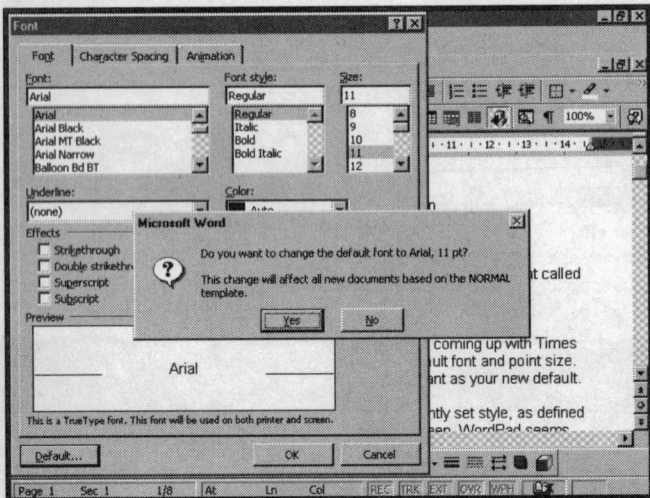

A If you do not like Word (or Works word processor) constantly coming up with Times New Roman 10 point when you load it, you can alter the default font and point size. Go to Format, Font, and select the font and point size you want as your new default.

In Word you will find that the new default will be for the currently set style, as defined in the style drop down list at the top left-hand side of your screen. WordPad seems utterly reluctant to allow you to change the default font, and don't even contemplate asking Notepad, which is a very basic text editor which just uses one fixed font.

There are many users who are reluctant to try different typefaces, or who have not bothered to explore the alternatives to Times or Arial. Do take a few moments out to click on the drop down list of typefaces and explore

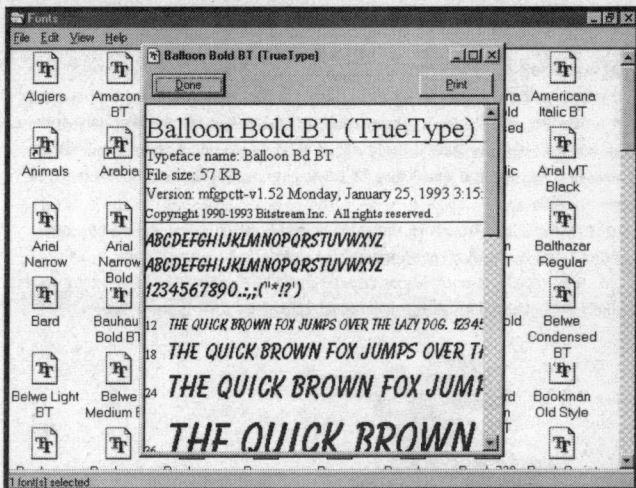

their effect.

You may well find that a judicious mix of different faces will greatly enhance your documents, but don't go mad and include more than three or four faces on a page, because that can make the page look cluttered, messy, and diffi-

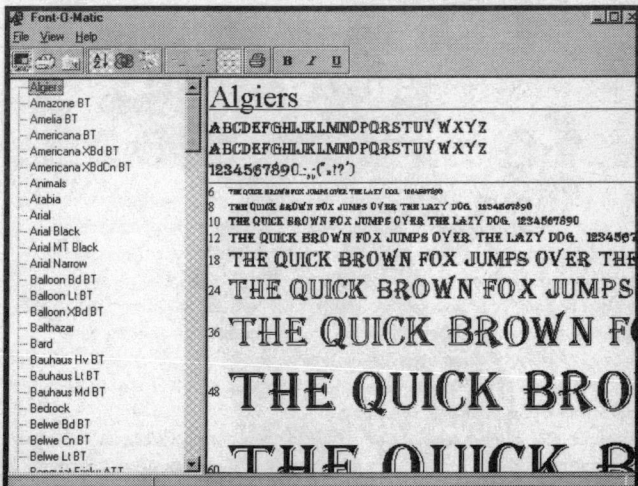

cult to read.

To get a preview of what fonts look like, go to Settings, Control Panel, Fonts and right click on the font you want. Then opt for Open. Do note that when you open a second or third font, you haven't got rid of the ones previously opened - they are just hidden behind the current window, so you should close them individually. Alt+F4 is a quick way of tidying up, as it closes the current window or application.

There is a neat little freeware program called Font-O-Matic, which can be obtained from its author by emailing him at hdeiner@myself.com, or at his site at www.geocities.com/SiliconValley/Park/2247/index.htm. It displays fonts, installed and otherwise, either alphabetically or by font type or family.

ALTERNATIVE EURO

Q When you discussed the Euro character earlier, you gave the keyboard combination as right-hand Alt+4. Isn't there an easier way? I'm not too good with Shift keys and the like. Also, how do you get over the problem when using a font which doesn't have the Euro?

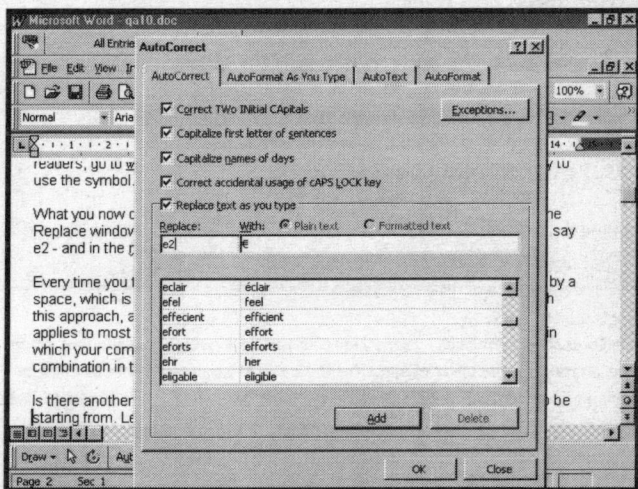

A There is a very simple solution for those few fonts which feature the Euro. For new readers, go to www.microsoft.com/windows/euro.asp if you want to download the ability to use the symbol. The fonts are Times New Roman, Arial and Comic Sans. If you have Windows 98, open Word, ensure you are using Times New Roman, and press Ctrl+Alt+4 - you may have the Euro symbol already.

What you now do is to go to Tools, Autocorrect. On the Autocorrect tab, click in the Replace window and type a short keyboard combination you don't normally use - say e2, for instance.

Every time you type e2 followed by a space, up comes the Euro symbol, followed by a space, which is a bit of a nuisance. However, there is a much bigger problem with this approach. If you are using a font without the Euro on it - and that applies to most of them - you simply get an out-line box character, which is the way in which your computer tells you that there isn't a character assigned to that key combination in the currently

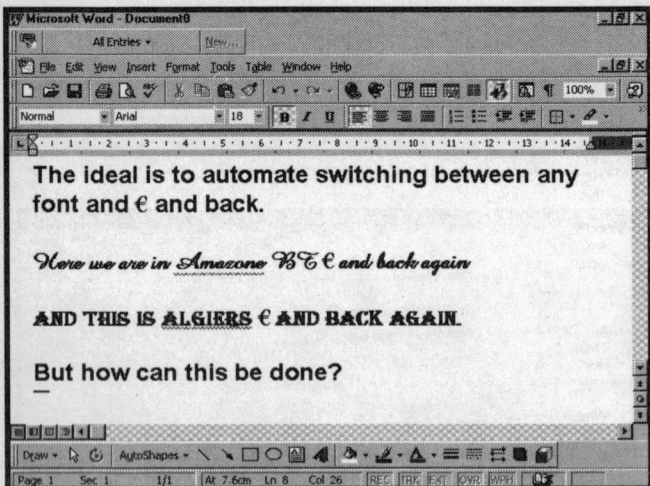

The ideal is to automate switching between any font and € and back.

Here we are in Amazone BT € and back again

AND THIS IS ALGIERS € AND BACK AGAIN

But how can this be done?

selected font.

Is there another approach? Yes, so long as you know which font you are going to be starting from. Let us assume for the sake of argument that your font of choice is Americana BT, which doesn't have the Euro symbol. First, ensure that

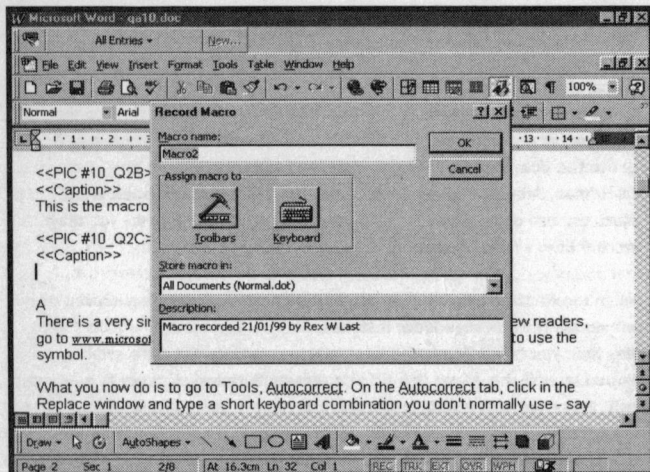

<<PIC #10_Q2B>
<<Caption>>
This is the macro

<<PIC #10_Q2C=
<<Caption>>

A
There is a very si..ew readers,
go to www.microso...to use the
symbol.

What you now do is to go to Tools, Autocorrect. On the Autocorrect tab, click in the Replace window and type a short keyboard combination you don't normally use - say

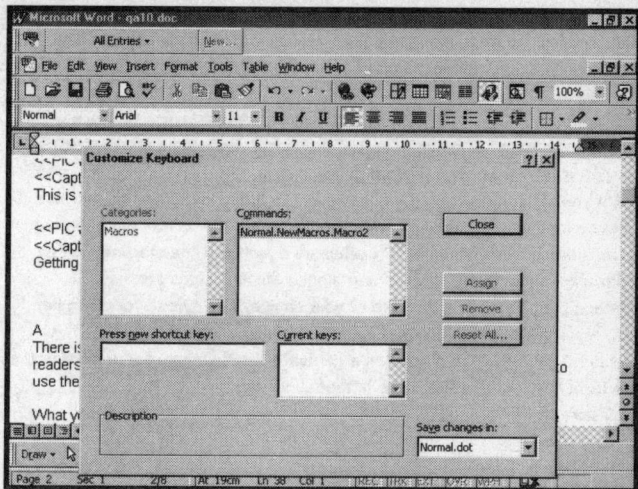

you are using Americana BT. Then go to Tools, Macro, Record macro. A macro
is a sequence of frequently carried out steps which can be repeated by
pressing a single key combination or a toolbar button. Sounds a bit off-
putting, but it is quite easy, so long as you follow the instructions.
At this stage, your next choice is to select a keyboard combination (Alt+ a
key, Shift+ a key, Ctrl+ a key, and so on) which is not otherwise in use, or to
opt to have the macro placed on a toolbar as a button.
Be careful when using keyboard combinations. Word will tell you that Alt+E
is not in use, but that means it isn't in use by another macro - it doesn't
warn you that you will get into bother every time when you press Alt+E to
get to the Edit menu!
Once your choice has been made, a little dialog box appears, allowing you to
abandon the macro recording process if something goes wrong, or to tell
Word that you have finished by clicking on the square symbol.

As you move the mouse pointer around the screen, you will see that, when it
is over the document window, it turns into a fairish imitation of a cassette.
This indicates that recording is currently in progress.
Now, open the drop-down list of fonts, locate Arial and click on it. Next, press
right Alt+4 (or Ctrl+Alt+4) to put the Euro character on the keyboard, then
open the fonts list again and click on Americana BT.
Click on the square, and you have your macro. Now press the key combination or click on your toolbar button and - lo and behold - you have a macro

which switches to Arial, prints the Euro, and then goes back to Americana BT.
You will need a separate macro for each font you want to use in this way.

If you go to Macros and Edit, you will see that you have, in effect, created a
short program in Visual BASIC which carries out the sequence of steps which
you have generated when you created the macro, and which you can edit and
change - if you know what you are doing, that is.

Now, if you are feeling brave, you can edit this little program to ensure that it
works no matter what font you are currently using. This is how it's done. Add a
line at the beginning of the text (make sure it isn't the line starting with an
apostrophe, since that's for comments only) which assigns the
Selection.Font.Name to a variable of your choice, say Myfont, for example.
Then, replace the last line with a line which assigns Myfont back to
Selection.Font.Name. That creates a general-purpose macro for accessing the
Euro from any font you like. Here is the full listing:

```
Sub Macro1()
'
' Macro1 Macro
' Macro recorded 18/01/99 by A N Other
'
    Myfont = Selection.Font.Name
    Selection.Font.Name = "Times New Roman"
    Selection.TypeText Text:="(type in the Euro symbol here)"
    Selection.Font.Name = Myfont
End Sub
```

If you want to use the Arial or Comic Sans version of the Euro symbol, replace
the font name Times New Roman with the name you want. As you will probably
have gathered, you can modify this technique to use with any character or
combination of characters.

POSTER POWER

Q I designed a poster in Word 97 for our gardening club and emailed it to a colleague's office, where they kindly agreed to duplicate a few copies for us. Unfortunately, it came out as garbage, because they had an earlier version of Word. I discovered that I could save the document in Word 6 format, which resolves that issue. But then he rang me up and told me that my splendid typeface came out as a quite different font. In the end I had to print it out and post it to him. Help!

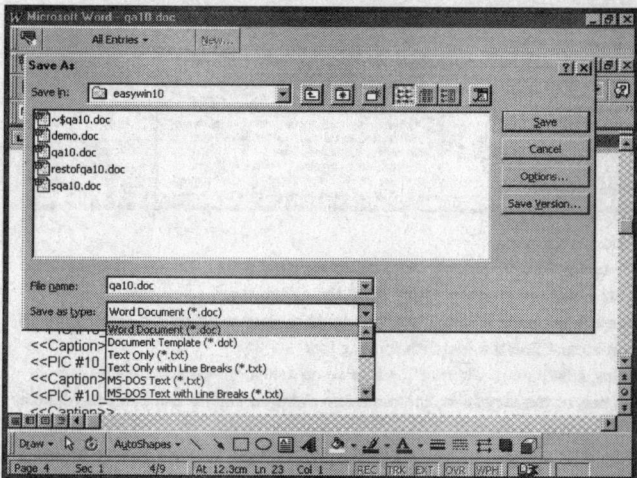

A That demonstrates Murphy's Law working at full power. Briefly, to explain the first problem which you solved by yourself: you can save Word documents in a variety of ways, but depending on the format, you may lose some or even all of your formatting.

If you have a feature unique to Word 97 and try to save that in Word 6 (or any earlier version) you will lose that feature, with unpredictable results. At the other extreme, if you save a document as a text file, you will lose all formatting and images.

You may be unsure as to where the document will end up. In that case, try saving it in more than one format: RTF (Rich Text Format) reproduces most Word formatting. MS-DOS Text with Layout tries to imitate the layout of a Word file. Look down the drop-down list to see what's there, and check, if possible, what the destination computer is and what word processor (and what

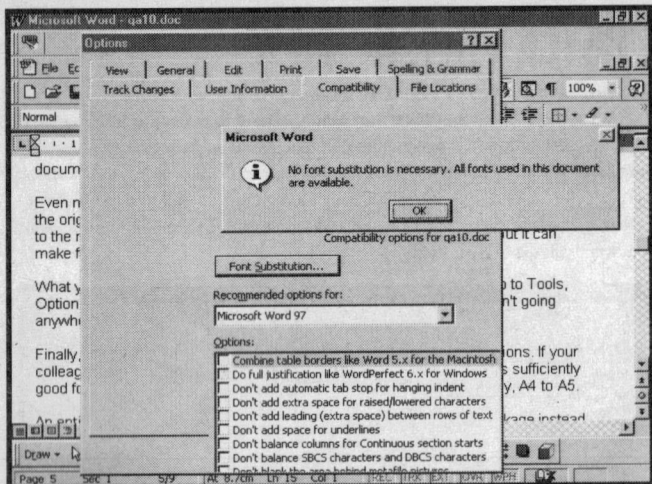

Screenshot: Microsoft Word - qa10.doc, Options dialog

Tabs: View | General | Edit | Print | Save | Spelling & Grammar
Track Changes | User Information | Compatibility | File Locations

Microsoft Word dialog:
No font substitution is necessary. All fonts used in this document are available.
[OK]

Compatibility options for qa10.doc

[Font Substitution...]

Recommended options for:
Microsoft Word 97

Options:
- [ ] Combine table borders like Word 5.x for the Macintosh
- [ ] Do full justification like WordPerfect 6.x for Windows
- [ ] Don't add automatic tab stop for hanging indent
- [ ] Don't add extra space for raised/lowered characters
- [ ] Don't add leading (extra space) between rows of text
- [ ] Don't add space for underlines
- [ ] Don't balance columns for Continuous section starts
- [ ] Don't balance SBCS characters and DBCS characters

Page 5   Sec 1   5/9   At 8.7cm   Ln 15   Col 1

version) it's running.

Now for the second part of your double-whammy. When you save a Word document, it obviously makes a note of all the different fonts you have used, and
when you reload it, it looks for those fonts on your machine. So, what happens
when it can't find the fonts it's looking for?

It tries substituting a 'similar' font. In some cases, that doesn't cause a problem, but, at the very least, there may be awkward page breaks that didn't occur
in the original document and other bits and pieces that will need tidying up.
Even more baffling, you will find that the font dialog box still contains the name
of the original font. The explanation for this is that the document may well be
going back to the machine it was first typed on after you had your go at revising
it, but it can make for a confusing situation.

If you want to override the choice of alternative font, go to Tools, Options,
Compatibility and click on Font Substitution. If the document isn't going anywhere else, you can opt to make the font change permanent.

Finally, if you are having problems of this kind, you can also consider two other
options. If your colleague has a plain paper fax, you may well find that a faxed
master is sufficiently good for reproduction purposes, particularly if you are
reducing from, say, A4 to A5.

An entirely different approach is to create a poster using a graphics package
instead, and then text and images will all be in the same format and will transfer
across to any other package which can read the appropriate format. There are
also format conversion programs available which will resolve most problems.

190

UPGRADING DISASTER

Q Help! I got an upgrade from my local computer shop in the form of a 2.1Gb hard drive, and now I seem to have lost some of my fonts which I know are on the CD-ROM which is sitting more or less permanently in the drive. What is going on?

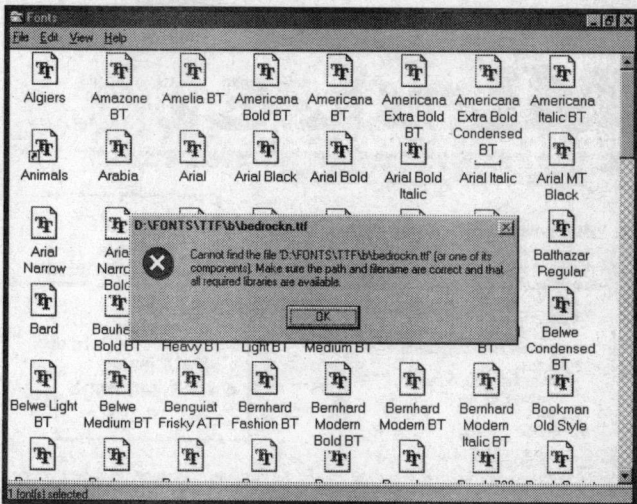

A What has happened is that the shop has taken the additional hard drive and called it D:, shifting the CD-ROM up the alphabet to drive E:. However, the shortcuts in your Fonts folder all seem to be pointing at drive D!

The simplest solution is to set aside some time to look through the shortcuts in the Fonts folder. Make a note of those which pointed to D:, and then delete them. Then, open up the CD-ROM and copy a shortcut to the fonts to the Windows Fonts folder. It will give you a chance to clear out unwanted fonts and add new ones, too.

To find out if a shortcut in the Fonts folder points to a non-existent file, double click on it. If nothing happens, it's a dud. Alternatively, right click on it and click Properties. You will get an error message if it's pointing to nowhere in particular.

To inspect a font before installing it, double click on it to bring up a window illustrating the font's features.

191

YOU'VE BEEN FRAMED!

Q I'm trying to get the hang of frames in Web pages. I can put up two frames, one on the left which is fixed and contains the links for the site, and the main part of the page contains the images and text. Trouble is, when I click on a link, the whole left-hand frame disappears. Help!

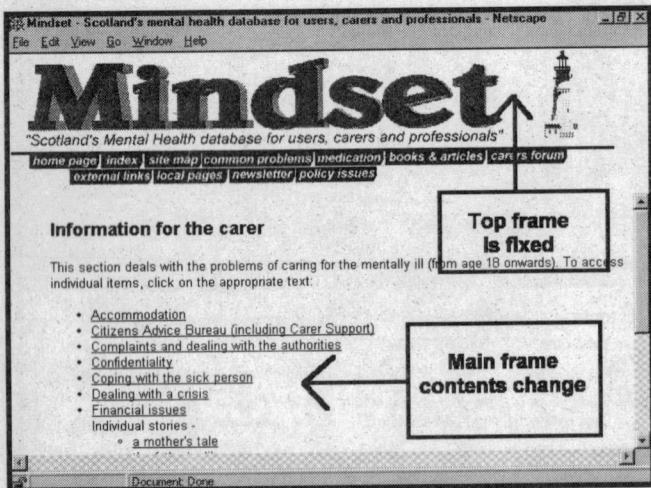

A A quick word of explanation about frames. They are used to divide the screen up into discrete sections, and are commonly used as an aid to navigation. One small part of the screen, usually at the left or top, contains links to the site, and remains constant wherever you go in the site. The rest of the screen is set aside for the pages of the site.

It's a clever concept, and one which can enormously enhance the appearance of your site, but as our reader indicates, it is more than a little fiddly to set up. If you have the facilities to download sites or to archive your cache, you may well find that the best way to proceed is to find a site with a setup similar to the one you want and 'borrow' the concept.

If you balked at the words 'archive your cache', don't panic! It merely means that unless you specify otherwise, recently visited sites are stored in a cache to speed up the appearance of pages on the screen. To unscramble the contents of the cache you need a special program.

There's a neat shareware program called Unmozify, which converts the cache

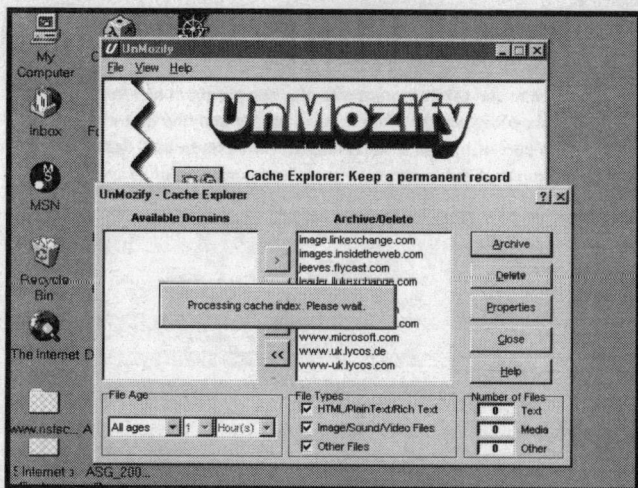

contents or selections from it into HTML files readable by Internet Explorer, and that can be accessed from their web site: www.nearsite.com

When you create a frame using FRAMESET, you then need to specify the source file for the frame using <FRAME SRC= >, and so on. Inside that tag, you create a name for each frame, such as NAME="left" and NAME="restof-screen".

Now, when you want to link to another file, you put the link in the <A HREF="filename.htm"> tag, but you also have to add the attribute: TAR-GET="restofscreen". That tells the program not to take over the whole screen, but to target it solely in the area occupied by that frame. The problem should now be solved.

If you want to wipe out the whole contents of the screen, which you may do if you are jumping to a different site altogether, add TARGET="_top".

ON THE MOVE WITH SPIKE

Q In Word, can you take different bits of a file, put them together and move them somewhere else? I often have to do this and find that it is rather tedious. What I do is to open a blank file, copy the bits to that, select all, and then copy to the Clipboard and paste back in the original file. Is that wrong?

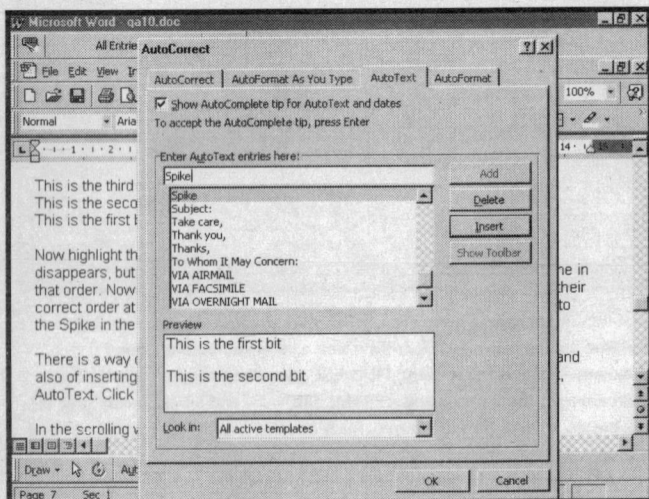

A Point one: Nothing that works is wrong. It may well be a more long-winded method than the fastest and most efficient approach, but if it works, don't knock it.

However, there is a way of doing what you want in Word. In fact, there is a way of getting Word to do just about everything except take the dog for a walk and make the tea - rumour has it that they are working on that too.

The feature in question is the Spike, which sounds painful, and which in fact may have been for all aspiring journalists in the old days of hot metal type-setting. It was literally a metal spike on to which sub-editors impaled material which they deemed unfit for publication. It was the newspaper equivalent of the film industry's cutting room floor.

Using the name Spike is a bit odd, to say the least, as Word's Spike is designed to hold material for later use rather than operate as a waste bin. To try the Spike out, type three or four separate lines of text, say:

This is the third bit
This is the second bit
This is the first bit

Now highlight the 'This is the first bit' text and press Ctrl+F3. The highlighted line disappears, but don't worry, it hasn't been lost. Do the same with lines two and one in that order. Now press Shift+Ctrl+F3, and - lo and behold - the three lines appear in their correct order at the point where the cursor was active. Note that the items go on to the Spike in the order in which you highlight them.

There is a way of viewing the Spike, or at least the first few lines of its contents, and also of inserting them without instantly deleting them from the Spike. Go to Insert, then AutoText. Click on the AutoText tab, and then on the AutoCorrect tab.

In the scrolling window, go down to the word Spike and highlight it. If there is anything on the Spike, you will see the first part of its contents in the preview window. Double click on the word Spike and it will appear in your document at the insertion point, without being erased this time.

Here is a special tip, which isn't to be found in Help, and which I discovered while typing this answer. If you type the first four letters of 'Spike', and there is something on it, you will see a small hint panel with the first part of the contents.

Press Enter and the contents are copied at the cursor (and the first letters of the word Spike are neatly dispensed with). The contents of the Spike are not deleted. The only nuisance is that it spills out a couple of unnecessary Enters after the phrase.

One other trick is that, if you are writing a document with a chunk of text, such as a title, or a complicated technical term, which you keep repeating, put it on the spike and you can recall it with the first four letters of the word 'Spike' as often as you like without prejudicing the contents of the Clipboard whatsoever.

Incidentally, this answer probably points to the solution of part of another reader's problem. She wrote saying that she was going for a particular key combination, missed, and a chunk of highlighted text simply disappeared and there was no way she could find of getting it back.

She was probably going for Shift+F3, which changes highlighted text from all caps, via all lower case to first letter of each word caps, and so on. She must have hit Ctrl+F3 by mistake and unwittingly 'spiked' her text.

One of the side effects of the complexity of Word is that baffling problems like this can arise from time-to-time. In such circumstances, do not forget the typist's best friend: Alt+E, and U for Undo. Word can undo up to 100 previous actions.

ON THE CHANGE...

Q There is a point which is puzzling me - How is it that my applications, when I switched from Windows 3.1 to 95, also changed the format of their load, save and other dialog boxes? Did they know about 95 in advance?

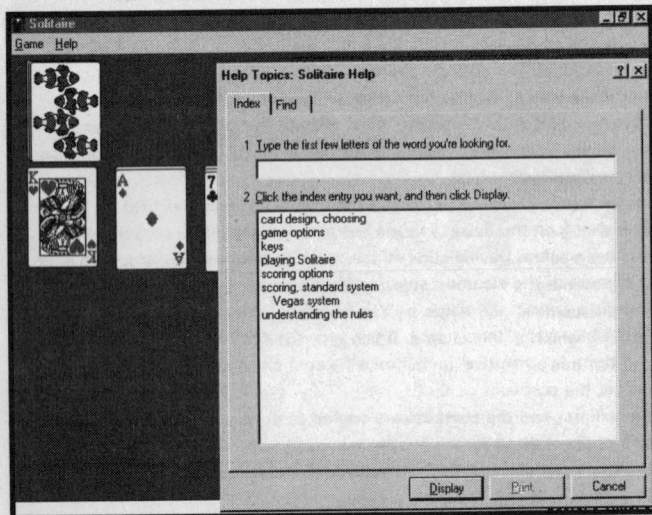

A That's a very intriguing question and one that may puzzle a lot of folk, so here goes with an attempt at an answer. Let's start with the assumption that you are sitting in MS-DOS mode and type, say, Notepad. You will promptly receive an abrupt message to the effect that this program requires Windows in order to run.

In other words, to cut a long story short, the program depends on Windows for all the bits and pieces which get it on to the screen, including the window or windows it needs, scrollbars, typefaces, colours and the rest. Also, it will use Windows dialog boxes for opening, saving, saving as, and so forth. In addition, features like menu bars are controlled by Windows, as is the Help facility which comes with the program. So, it's rather like a car manufacturer taking a chassis, engine, and so on, and fitting different bodies on top. The essential workings are the same, but the external appearance changes. Even the radically different appearance of Help (at least in Windows 95) takes the same basic files and presents them in a different way.

A BACKUP CALAMITY

Q I am not sure what happened, but the other day I seem to have lost the entire contents of a valuable backup disk. I inserted it into the drive, typed DIR A: (using the MS-DOS Window), and found the list of files for the last disk I'd inserted coming up instead of the current disk. There was no way I could get the listing back, so I had lost an entire backup. What's happening?

A Golden rule number one: Whenever you have archived material on a floppy disk, flick the plastic square slider upwards so that there is a clear square gap visible. That protects the disk against being overwritten. Only close the slider when you specifically want to add material to the disk or change its contents.

As to what has happened in your case, you have fallen victim to a rather nasty little catch which you should be wary of. If you type DIR A: in the MS-DOS window as you are inserting a disk, the system may still think it's the previous disk, and it may also overwrite the file allocation table of that disk, which it still has stored in memory.

If the FAT has been overwritten, the irony is that your files are still actually there, but may now be totally inaccessible, because the contents of files can be scattered all over the disk and can only be read if these locations can be properly tracked.

The alternative explanation, particularly if this problem occurs on a regular basis, is that the floppy drive may be in terminal decline. The good news is that a replacement drive is ridiculously cheap nowadays, less than twenty pounds in fact. That's a far cry from the old days when a floppy drive for a BBC Micro - single density, single sided, 5.25 inch - was hundreds of pounds.

DODGY SCREENSAVERS

Q I loaded a screensaver from a CD-ROM and it caused my screen to go completely bananas. After a struggle, I managed to get the computer going in safe mode but after I'd saved all my files I had to reload Windows 95 from scratch. What caused this?

A First, find a waste paper bin and insert the CD-ROM securely in it. No, seriously: some of those screen savers and other such programs really do need a clear government health warning on them. What happened was that, during the installation process, you were asked an apparently innocent question about installing screen drivers.

You probably thought no more about it, but agreed to have them installed, and that's where the trouble came from. What I guess has happened is that the screen drivers on the CD-ROM were in fact older versions than the ones on your machine, and that is why everything crashed. At the very least, they were entirely inappropriate.

If you must have silly screen savers, do not - repeat, NOT - agree to have the screen drivers upgraded unless you are absolutely sure of what you are doing. Most folk would rather do without a Simpsons or a Porsche screen saver than spend hours trying to undo the damage.

THE LONG AND SHORT OF IT

Q How does MS-DOS cope with long file names? And what are all these squiggly bits in the names?

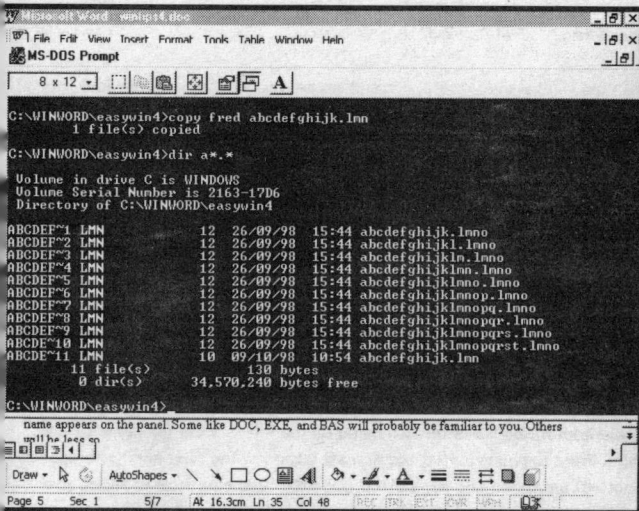

```
Microsoft Word - winigs4.doc                                    _ 6 X
File  Edit  View  Insert  Format  Tools  Table  Window  Help    _ 8 x
MS-DOS Prompt                                                   _ 8

 8 x 12 ▾

C:\WINWORD\easywin4>copy fred abcdefghijk.lmn
        1 file(s) copied

C:\WINWORD\easywin4>dir a*.*

 Volume in drive C is WINDOWS
 Volume Serial Number is 2163-17D6
 Directory of C:\WINWORD\easywin4

ABCDEF~1 LMN            12  26/09/98  15:44 abcdefghijk.lnno
ABCDEF~2 LMN            12  26/09/98  15:44 abcdefghijkl.lnno
ABCDEF~3 LMN            12  26/09/98  15:44 abcdefghijklm.lnno
ABCDEF~4 LMN            12  26/09/98  15:44 abcdefghijklnn.lnno
ABCDEF~5 LMN            12  26/09/98  15:44 abcdefghijklmnno.lnno
ABCDEF~6 LMN            12  26/09/98  15:44 abcdefghijklmnnop.lnno
ABCDEF~7 LMN            12  26/09/98  15:44 abcdefghijklmnnopq.lnno
ABCDEF~8 LMN            12  26/09/98  15:44 abcdefghijklmnnopqr.lnno
ABCDEF~9 LMN            12  26/09/98  15:44 abcdefghijklmnnopqrs.lnno
ABCDE~10 LMN            12  26/09/98  15:44 abcdefghijklmnnopqrst.lnno
ABCDE~11 LMN            10  09/10/98  10:54 abcdefghijk.lmn
       11 file(s)           130 bytes
        0 dir(s)      34,570,240 bytes free

C:\WINWORD\easywin4>
```

```
name appears on the panel. Some like DOC, EXE, and BAS will probably be familiar to you. Others
will be less so
Draw ▾  ☐ ⚪  AutoShapes ▾  \  ⟍  ☐ ○ ▢ ◢ ▣  ⟐ ▾ ✎ ▾ △ ▾ ≡ ≡ ⇄ ⬛ ⬙
Page 5   Sec 1    5/7    At 16.3cm Ln 35  Col 48   REC TRK EXT OVR WPH
```

A This is one of those short questions with a long answer, one that reveals more than the odd anomaly in the way in which long file names work. To begin with, before Windows 95, the file name was restricted to 8.3 characters, with eight letters before the full stop (which is put there just for the sake of us humans) and up to three after in the extension, or file type. That explains why labels have 11 characters - they are a special variation on a file name.

Those three characters after the notional full stop are quite often reserved for special purposes. To see what file types are associated with what characters, open My Computer, click on View, Options, and the File types tab. To find out what type goes with what kind of file, scroll down to the file of your choice and click on it. The extension name appears on the panel. Some like DOC, EXE, and INI will probably be familiar to you. Others will be less so.

Windows 95 introduced the concept of long file names. And, in order to be backwards compatible with a raft of MS-DOS operations and programs designed for 3.1x, which had to continue to run on 95, some way had to be devised of expressing long file names in the 8.3 format.

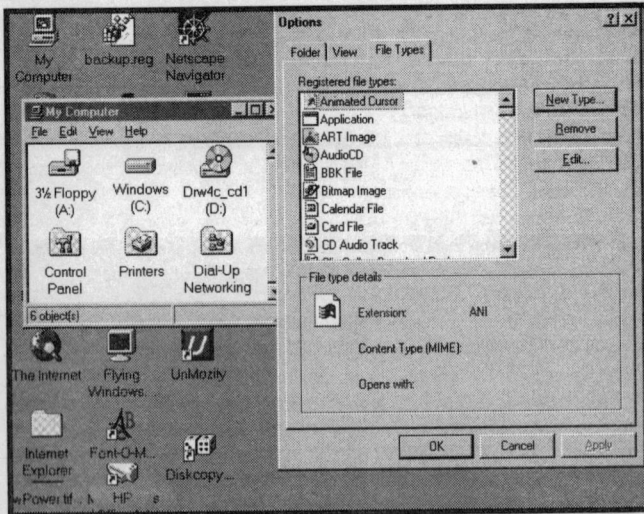

For the easiest way to see how MS-DOS manages, do a DIR listing in a MS-DOS Window. You'll see the 8.3 name on the left and the full name on the right. What happens is that the first six letters of the file name (with spaces omitted) are taken and capitalised. Then the tilde character is added (the squiggle to which you so eloquently refer), followed by a number in the range 1 to 9.

If there are two files whose first six characters are identical, they will be referred to, for example, as ABCDEF~1.COM and ABCDEF~2.COM. If there are more than nine files in that category, the tenth file will be called ABCDE~10.COM.

Given the flexibility accorded to the user, including the use of multiple full stops, the system copes with it all pretty well. However, there are a few anomalies lurking in the undergrowth. One of them has to do with DEL, which allows you to delete files, and can be pretty nasty if you are not aware of it.

DEL *.XXX

gets rid of all files whose extension begins with the characters XXX.

There is also an odd quirk in REN, which renames a file. If you have a file with a four-letter extension, like JPEG for example, the first of these commands won't work, but the second will:

REN FRED.JPE FRED.JPG
REN *.JPE *.JPG

In order to overcome this little glitch - sorry, feature - you need to enclose the name in quotes (which is also necessary if the file name contains a space, as in CD "program files"):

REN "FRED.JPEG" FRED.JPG

EDIT allows you to create files with long names and, for the most part, all goes well - but it is best to be cautious if you are carrying out any operations which involve deleting or renaming.

And a final reminder: there are applications written for Windows 3.1 which can cause havoc with long file names, especially if they are system utilities and don't recognise the long names at all.

CUSTOMISING AUTOCORRECT

Q I want to have a series of lines automatically typed, the lines of my address. However, Autocorrect will only allow me to type in a single continuous line. What's going on?

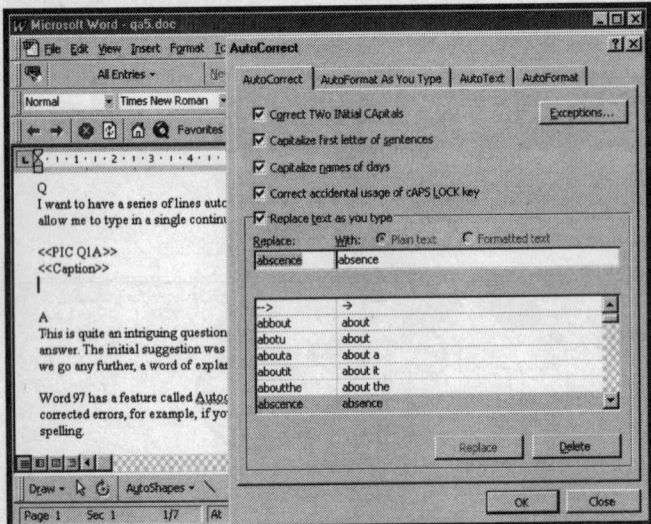

A Autocorrect is an extremely powerful feature of Word. Not only does it offer a built-in list of common typing errors which it corrects automatically (unless you switch the feature off), you can also customise error correction, and the beneficial side-effect is that you can persuade Word to convert a short sequence of characters you are not likely to use in the text - A1, A2, or A3, for example - into a string of characters of varying length. This helps to speed up your typing and is particularly beneficial for those who for whatever reason find typing difficult.

However, the problem is to work out how to include formatting in that string of characters. This is a bit of a tricky one and it took a while to fathom out what was going on. In the left-hand window of Autocorrect you are invited to type in text which will be replaced by what's in the right-hand window. However, it doesn't seem possible to enable the radio buttons which allow you to opt for formatted or plain text, so you are stuck with a single line. It took a couple of cups of coffee and some serious head-scratching to come up with the answer, which is pretty obvious and simple when you know it (aren't they all!). If, for example, you want a name and address typed out when you key in the characters 'A1' (followed by a space or Enter), open a new blank document and type the material line formatted line-by-line as you want it to appear.

Then press Alt+E, C to copy it to the Clipboard. Now when you summon up Autocorrect, you will find the address in the right-hand window ready and waiting for you. This technique can save you a lot of typing. The only thing to remember is not to use a sequence which you want for something else!

If you want to override Autocorrect, say you have automatic capitalisation of the first word in a sentence and you want a lower case letter after an exclamation mark, for instance, what you do is type the exclamation mark, followed by two spaces, then the left arrow key (not the left delete key). Now type the word, and Word will not change it, although it will still put a squiggly red underline if it doesn't like it for other reasons.

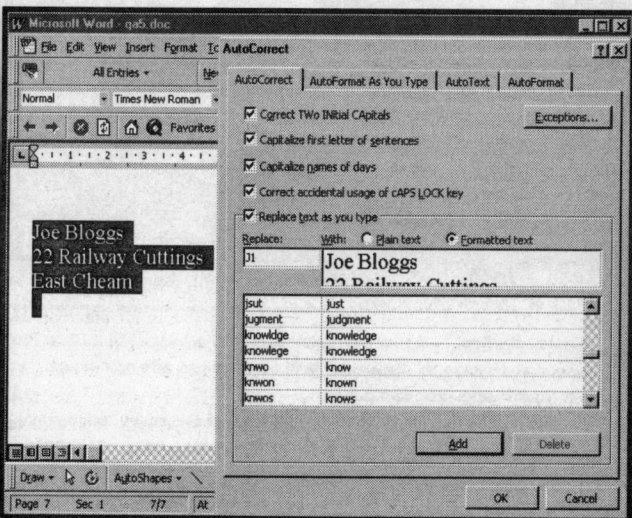

I WANT TO BE FRAMED!

Q I have Paint Shop Pro and I'd like to know how you get those fancy effects round an image like a frame, or the one that looks as if the outer edge of the image had been smoothly bent back. You often see this effect on stills on the TV news, and also on Internet pages. How do they do that? And, even more important, how can I get to do that?

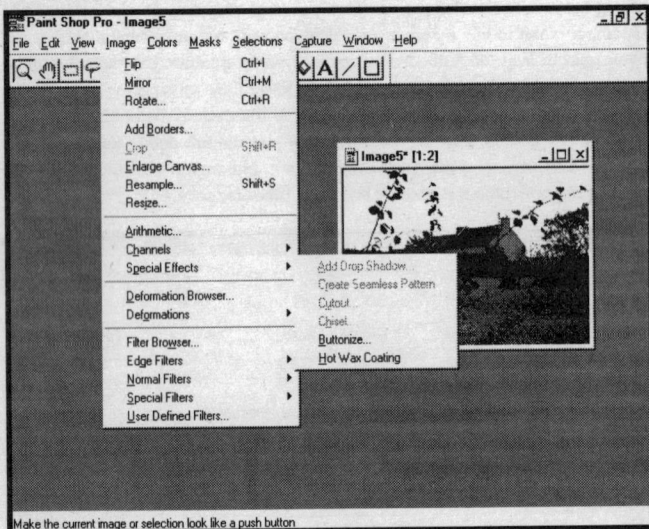

A The fanciest effect is in fact the simplest one to achieve. Paint Shop Pro has special effects and distortions built in which can add drama and interest to your images and web pages.

The one which makes the image seem to curl back at the edges, so to speak, is the Buttonize effect. This is a very powerful technique, not least because you are able to vary the amount of stretch at the edges. Simply go to Image and opt for Special effects, then Buttonize. Then adjust the figure in the preview window to see how the effect will change the image.

Hot wax, another Special effect, needs a little more care and attention. First select which part of the image you want to change (or you can opt to change the whole image). Then decide which colour you want the effect to be based on. Use the Dropper to select the colour and experiment before you commit yourself. If you select an inappropriate colour, you may effectively black out-

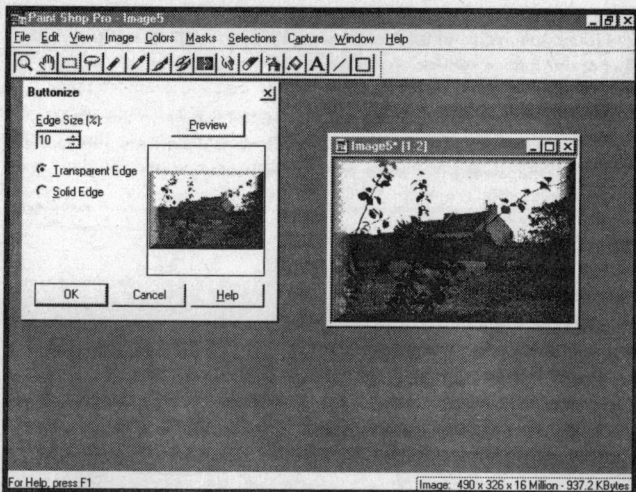

the entire image.

Another way of putting a border round an image is to use the Chisel effect.
The best way to achieve this is to open a new image bigger than the one
you want to give a border to, select the whole of your existing image, then

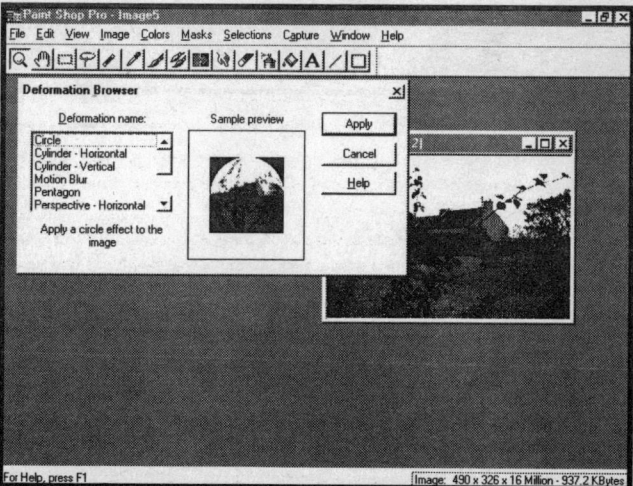

paste it into the middle of the blank image. Now go for Chisel and try out the effect of the various settings. Try different colours for the border by opting for Background colour rather than Transparent.

There are also a number of distortions on offer. You can watch the effect each has by using the Deformation browser. Combine distortions with special effects and you can arrive at some pretty eye-catching results.

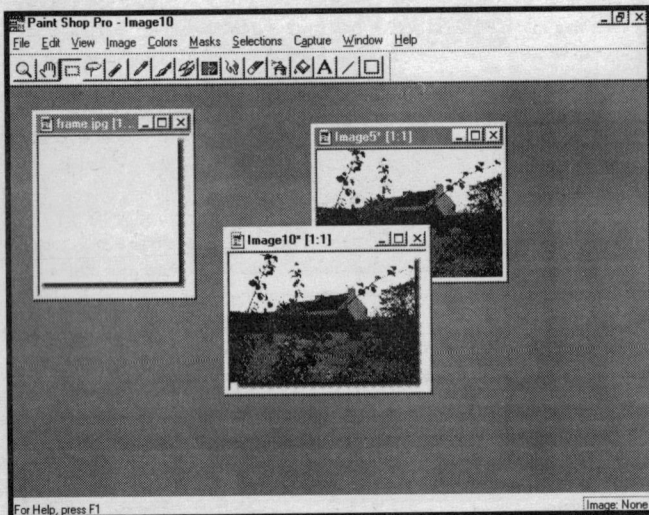

TAKE NOTE

Q What's the easiest way of opening Notepad without having to hack my way through various folders? Also, why can't I get Notepad to work with some text files?

A The first problem here is that when you open Notepad, it will insist in starting in the Windows folder, and you have to go hopping and skipping around to where you want to go, or you have to type the full path name to get at the file. Not a convenient set of options, you must agree.

You could, of course, put the files you want to edit in the Windows folder, but that isn't advisable. It is always best to create your own folders for your own documents to avoid confusion and, worse still, accidentally deleting system files.

Instead of opening Notepad and then going off on a merry chase for the file you want, the way to deal with the situation is to tackle it the other way round, so to speak. First, as Mrs Beeton might have said, find your file, or rather, the folder in which the file you want is sitting.

From My Computer or Explorer, right click on the folder you want, then opt for Open MS-DOS Window here. When the prompt appears, type NOTEPAD followed by the filename you want, or by itself to open a new Notepad file. You can perform a number of similar operations directly from the ancient panes of the MS-DOS Window, if the Path in the Autoexec.bat file includes the directory where they are located, and if you know what the MS-DOS names of the programs are. Also, you obviously need to have them loaded on your system. Check Help, Add/Remove programs if you haven't.

For example, typing CLIPBRD at the MS-DOS prompt will open the Clipbook viewer, so you can see what's on the Clipboard and perform other operations. Type CHARMAP and up pops the Character Map.

MSHEARTS gets the game of Hearts going and SOL cranks up Solitaire. If you are really feeling withdrawal symptoms from Windows 3.x, typing PROG-MAN brings up the old Program Manager. And TASKMAN unveils the Task Manager.

Alternatively, go for Start, Run and type the appropriate character sequence. Run has the advantage over MS-DOS in that it finds WordPad (just type WORDPAD) whereas MS-DOS won't, unless you are in the Accessories folder. To answer your second question: Notepad is restricted to 64K size for documents. For larger documents, use WordPad, but do remember that you must specifically ask for it to save the material as a text file if you don't want the document formatting and saving as a Word DOC file.

MINIMISE YOUR TROUBLES

Q I had a help panel open in Word. Then I typed Alt+F, O to open a file. The whole system seemed to freeze and I had to reboot. What was going on?

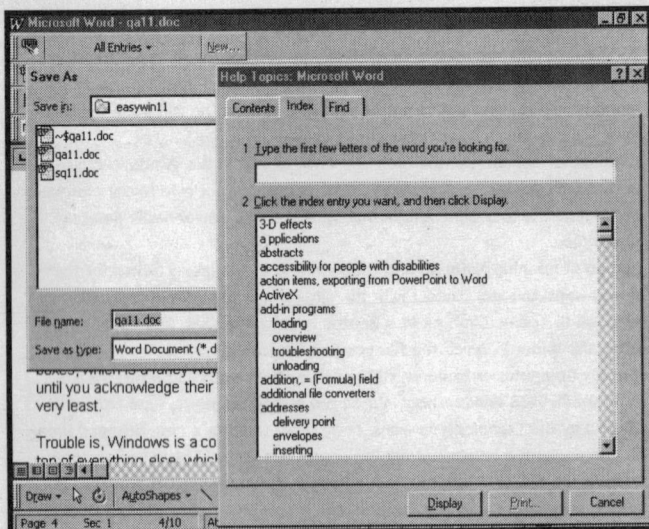

A The system hadn't frozen. This is a situation which can arise from time to time, and the explanation goes like this. Many windows are in the form of modal dialog boxes, which is a fancy way of saying that once they are open, they won't go away until you acknowledge their presence by pressing the OK or Cancel buttons at the very least.

Trouble is, Windows is a complicated beast, and Help panels by default appear on top of everything else, which most of the time is very useful if you are trying to follow advice step-by-step.

However, what happened in your case is that the Open File dialog box did appear, but it was hidden behind the Help panel. You could have progressed quite simply by minimising the Help panel. If you look at the Options menu on Help, you can choose whether or not to have Help on top all the time.

One neat trick which will tell you which modal dialog box is gumming up the works is to try and minimise all Windows, either by right clicking on an empty spot on the Taskbar and selecting the appropriate option, or if you have a Windows keyboard, pressing Win+M. The offending dialog box should then

DOS-WINDOWS DISKCOPY

Q I am a fan of the MS-DOS program Diskcopy, and wonder whether it's possible to run it from a Windows icon on the Desktop rather than from an MS-DOS Window. The real snag, as I see it, is that (a) I am not sure how to put it on the Desktop, and (b) is it possible to add the parameters A: A: to indicate that the copying should be from one disk to another? It's a neat way to make multiple backups, but can it be brought into the era of Windows?

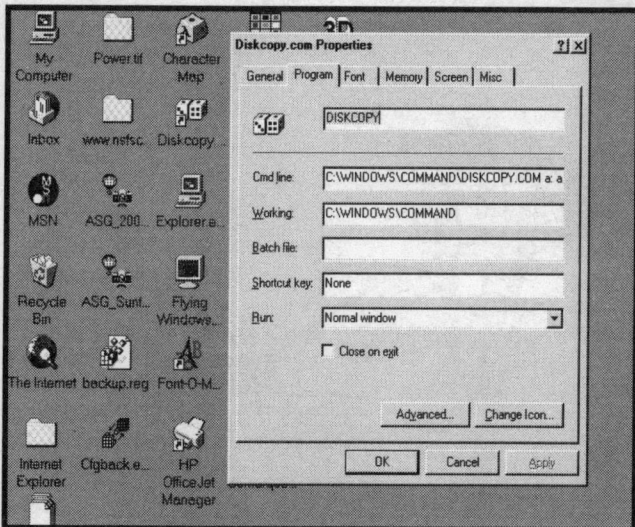

A It is quite possible to perform this little trick, but first just a word to people who may not generally consider using this MS-DOS program at all. You can use My Computer, File, then Copy Disk, but Diskcopy is fine so long as you don't mind taking the trouble to set it up.

What follows is valid for any MS-DOS program. First, find the program, which in this case will be on your hard disk in the DOS folder, which is in the root folder. Open the folder and locate Diskcopy.exe.

Now hold the right mouse button down and drag the icon to the Desktop. Create a shortcut on the Desktop, then right click on the icon and select Properties. Click on the Program tab.

Now add to the end of the command line a space, followed by A: another space and then A: again. Click screen and select window or full screen, depending on your preference. Nearly there.

If you want to change the icon, go to the Program tab again, then click on icons and choose the one which takes your fancy. Now, when you double click on the icon, you will get an MS-DOS window in which you are invited to insert the disk you want to copy from into drive A.

Maybe you don't feel that this is worth the trouble, but if, for example, you have QBASIC and a particular program you still want to run using that language, you can go through the above process adding to the command line the path of the program you want to run with it.

USING VISUAL BASIC

Q I am confused. Now I have Word 97 I see that you can make macros with something called Visual Basic. What happened to WordBasic and can I still use those macros on my new version?

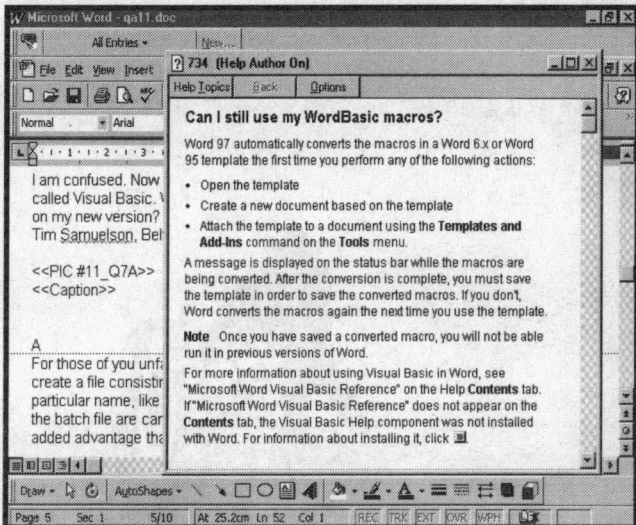

A For those of you unfamiliar with the term, a macro is like a batch file, where you create a file consisting of a series of instructions to the computer, save it with a particular name, like FRED.BAT. Next time you type FRED, the instructions inside the batch file are carried out as if you had typed them in one at a time. There's the added advantage that you can jump back and forward under given conditions, too. One batch file you may well have heard of is AUTOEXEC.BAT which runs automatically when the computer starts up.

The language of batch files was pretty restricted and fiddly to get right. Visual Basic, on the other hand, is a full-blown Windows programming language. Now to your question: WordBasic is the ancestor of Visual Basic, if you like. It is used with earlier versions of Word and has now been replaced by Visual Basic.

What happens when you open a template which contains a macro written in WordBasic is that Word will try and upgrade it to Visual Basic.

Check through the macro, and on lines where changes need to be made you'll see the term WordBasic.

A word of warning, though: once converted to Visual Basic, the macros won't make sense to earlier versions of Word; so, if you are working with anyone still using an earlier edition, ensure you keep a version of the template that they can understand.

SAVING CLIPPINGS

Q As I understand it, the Clipboard just contains the currently copied (or cut) image. Is it possible to have more than one image on the Clipboard without losing what's already there?

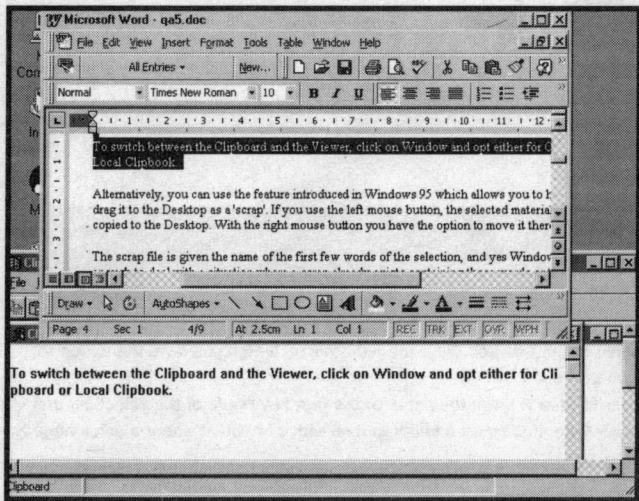

A Indeed you can, but you have to save any existing material first. If you have the Clipbook viewer on your Accessories continuation menu (install it, if you haven't), you can save Clipbook information in CLP files or as pages, which you can then load into the Clipboard and paste into your document. You can also share material with other users if you wish.

To access this feature, run the Clipboard. If you have currently got information pasted into the Clipboard you can view it on the Clipboard and, if you have two applications open, you can watch this happening in real time.

To save the information as a page or CLP file, opt for Save As. To create a page, go for Paste. To switch between the Clipboard and the Viewer, click on Window and either opt for Clipboard or Local Clipbook. For extra support, there is plenty of help is available for this utility. Just go for the Help menu option.

As an alternative to the Clipboard, you can use the feature introduced in Windows 95 which allows you to highlight text and drag it to the Desktop as a 'scrap'. If you use the left mouse button, the selected material is simply

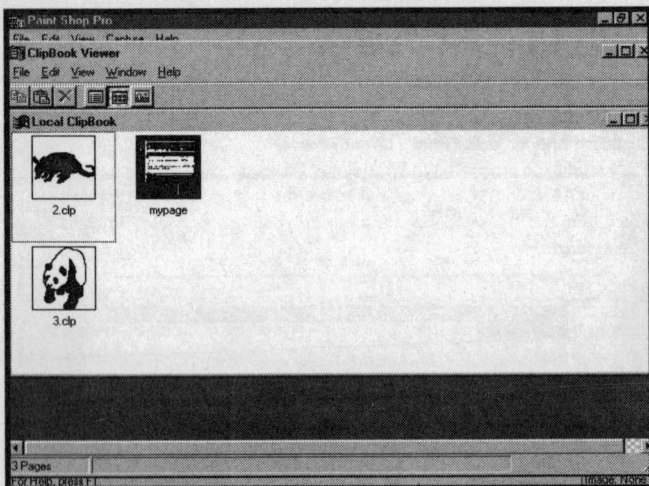

copied to the Desktop. With the right mouse button you have the option to
move it there.

The scrap file is given the name of the first few words of the selection, and -
yes - Windows is smart enough to deal with a situation where a scrap already

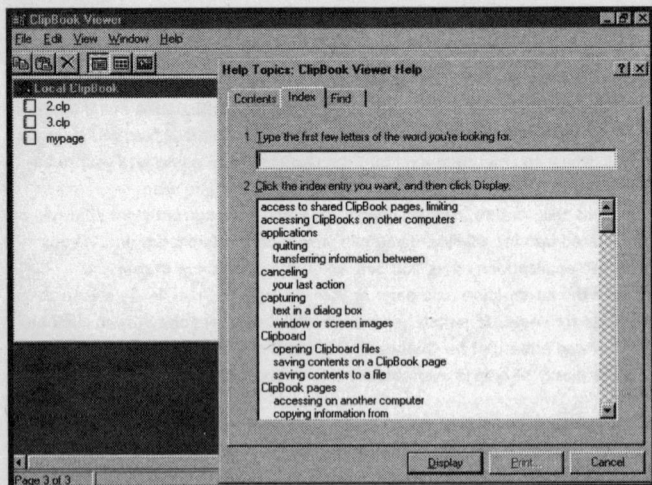

TWO COLUMNS, DOUBLE THE TROUBLE

Q I produce a newsletter in Word 2 and I'd like to change from single column A4 to double columns, but I have run into difficulties. How do I switch from two to one column for a heading and how do I keep columns even in length?

A Let me explain what causes the uneven columns in the first place. If you have text which doesn't take up exactly a page (and how often does that happen!), the first column goes to the bottom of the page and the rest goes to the second column, leaving a yawning gap. Even worse, you can get just a partial first column and the right-hand side of the page is left completely blank.

To create columns and keep them even, firstly select the text you want to have in two columns, then click just after the last character. At this point opt for Alt+I (Insert), then B for Break. Up pops a dialog box, and from the options select Continuous, then OK.

Now go to Alt+F, V to preview the page. If there is still some unevenness, you will probably find it is caused by an extra paragraph character or something similar. Click on the paragraph marker on your toolbar to show formatting features. That will help you work out how to even up the columns.

Finally, as ever, the advice is to get your text as near to completion as possible before laying it out as you want it, especially if you are after more complex layout effects such as two columns.

BAD BODY SPACING

Q I use Body text for my newsletter but the spacing between the lines keeps going wrong. Solution please!

A There are various different formats for spacing between the lines, which used to be called leading (pronounced to rhyme with Reading, not reading, if you see what I mean), named after the thickness of the piece of lead placed between the lines of type in the days of hot metal typesetting.

If the balance between the font size is wrong, the text can look either very crowded or spindly and thin, so the trick is to get the right combination of the two. Another part of the formula is the width of the line of text on the page. If you have ten point text running the full width of an A4 page, which, incidentally, has been shown by psychologists to be difficult for the eye to follow because it has to scan across a lot of text, then 'fly back' to the beginning of the next line. On the other hand, very narrow columns are equally difficult to read because the eye is flicking back and forth too quickly.

The final consideration is which font and which style to use. A serif font (one with curly bits round the edges of letters), like Times New Roman, is easier to read over long stretches of text than a sans serif, like Arial - although Arial is clean and quite striking for short items. Also, avoid a long section in italics, which makes for hard reading and is not particularly nice to look at.

After deciding on your font, settle on your line width and point size. For a newsletter, ten or eleven point is best and, regarding layout, two columns are most suitable. Note that Word 97 allows for uneven columns, which can be employed to striking effect.

If you find that the interline spacing is not satisfactory, highlight the text you want to change, go to Format, Paragraph and click on the Indents and spacing tab. You'll see an option to select Line spacing, which may be set to Auto, in which case the balance may well be just right. If you set it to At Least, try varying the point size to move lines nearer or further apart.

SEEING THROUGH THE PROBLEM

Q I have a banner at the top of each of the pages on my website. They are GIF files and Version 89a interlaced. They are on a white background and the background is transparent so that the text and image appear against my chosen background colour. However, the last one I set up just won't work. The area covered by the banner stays obstinately white. What have I done?

A Images make a web page more than just a collection of bits of information - it can become very attractive and pleasing on the eye. And that's important, especially if you want to grab the attention of a user who is surfing the net and will only stay with a page if it looks good.

The first item to check is that you have not inadvertently switched off the transparency setting. Open the image, go to Alt+F, then Save As. Click on Options and ensure that the correct radio button is set. Note that you can set the transparency value either to the original background colour, the current background colour or a palette setting of your choice.

When you edited this banner, presumably by putting some text or an image on it, the background colour when saved was not the one you wanted. This is an issue you should be aware of when using graphics packages - do be aware of the foreground and background colours, otherwise you can end up with all kinds of unintended results. It is very easy to lose track of which colours, fonts and tools you are using when working with complex graphics.

COLOURED LINKS

Q One of the things that mystifies me about websites is that, with many of them, the link actually changes colour when you have clicked on it and then return to the calling page. Even more mystifying is the fact that the computer or the website somehow 'remembers' that fact when I switch on the machine the next day and go for the same site. How do they do that?

A The HTML (HyperText Markup Language) code which underlies web pages can contain attributes called LINK, VLINK and ALINK. They determine the colour of the underlined text or border round an image which forms a link to another page. An unused link's colour is determined by LINK, a recently visited link by VLINK, and ALINK causes the link to change to that colour as you click on it.

These commands may not work with earlier versions of your browser. For HTML buffs, you will notice that I called them attributes rather than commands in their own right. They are in fact attributes of the BODY command, which comes near the beginning of the source code. The information about which links have been visited is stored on your hard disk in a cache.

COPYING, DOS-STYLE

Q Can you copy what's in an MS-DOS Window into a Windows program? I've tried using Copy and Paste in the MS-DOS editor and it doesn't work. Can you help?

A There are a couple of situations where the normal Copy, Cut and Paste operations won't work as expected in Windows. One of the most important aspects of the design of Windows and its applications is the aspiration to make everything uniform across the whole range, so to speak, so that if you press Alt+F, for example, up comes the File menu whatever the application.

For a whole raft of reasons, there are occasions when this won't work. Many word processors opt for Alt+S for Search and Replace, but Word requires Alt+E. Early versions of Word have Alt+E, A for Select All, later versions have Alt+E, L.

In the MS-DOS Window, you have to click on the icon at the top left-hand corner, let the mouse button hover over the Edit option and then go for Paste, which is fairly obviously allows you to import material, or Mark.

What Mark does is to put a square pointer in the top left-hand corner of the MS-DOS Window, which you then move to the start point you require. Hold down the mouse button, then drag the square to the size you require.

Note that you can even mark half a line of text if you wish; press Enter to Copy (or go to Edit, then copy) and switch over to your Windows application to paste it.

This rather remarkable (pun not intended) feature can be used directly from the MS-DOS prompt or from the EDIT program. One possible application is that if you receive a two or more column address list in hard copy and scan it in using OCR (Optical Character Recognition), you can actually split up the columns and reorganise the output to your requirements.

WHAT'S IN THE BOX?

Q Can you put a box round words or paragraphs in Word 97. If so, how?

A The text box is a long-standing feature of Word which has matured over the various versions to the point at which you can have multiple overlapping text boxes, which enables you to create newsletters with complex designs.

Starting from scratch, you activate the Drawing toolbar (Alt+V for View, then T for Toolbars) and click on Text Box. You will find a cross cursor, which you then take to one corner of your text box and then drag it to the size you want.

You can approach this the other way round, too, by selecting a chunk of text and going for Alt+O (Format) and Borders and shading.

For more advanced options available when working with sections of text, see the Newsletter Wizard.

Go to Alt+F for File, then New and click on the publications tab. If you don't have the Wizard, you will have to install it. For further information, see Wizards in Word Help.

THE PROBLEM WITH WIDOWS & ORPHANS

Q I don't like widows and orphans, but sometimes one appears at the top of a page. What can I do?

A To reassure other readers - no, this isn't Ebenezer Scrooge writing in. The first and most important point is that it's best to delay dealing with layout features like this until the text of the document has been finalised; this applies equally to hyphenating words to achieve a smoother inter-word spacing.

Another little problem that can occur if you have a blank line as a paragraph marker is that if you break at the top of a page, you'll have a paragraph starting a line further down than on other pages, and you need to deal with that manually.

There are two ways of achieving control of widows and orphans. You can have automatic widow and orphan control, which can be accessed via Paragraph. This prevents Word from printing a line by itself at the top of a page - that's called a widow - or the first line of a paragraph at the end of a page - an orphan, as you'll have no doubt guessed.

Another approach is to switch off control of widows and orphans, get to the point where you are putting the finishing touches to your text, and then see how you can manually improve the appearance of your text. This is particularly important if you have a sub-heading which appears at the bottom of a column. That looks particularly clumsy.

What you do is examine the text carefully and see if splitting a paragraph into two will resolve the problem. Adding a word or two or a short sentence may well do the trick. Remember, in a document which will be published, whether it be an internal memorandum, a newsletter or a full-blown book, appearances are vital.

There is nothing sacred about the words written either by yourself or the others who have contributed to the document. Readers will be far more irritated by layout problems than your writers will be by the odd judicious piece of cosmetic sub-editing.

WIPING OUT FILES

Q I have a problem. I was a bit short of space on my hard drive, so I deleted some big files. Now I can't get Works help to come up at all. What can I do?

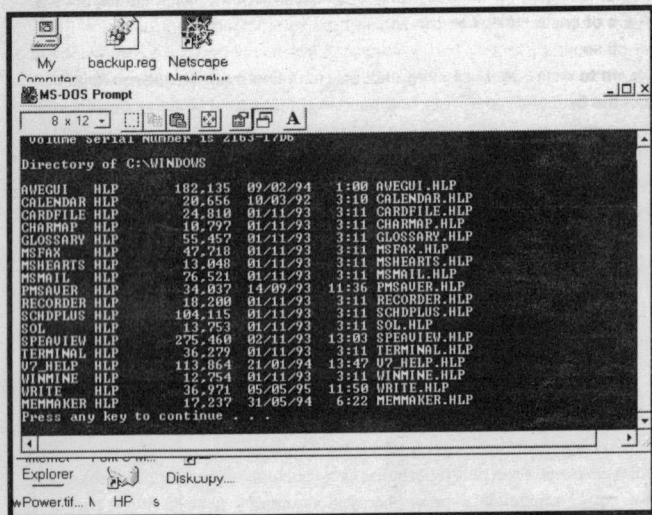

A There is a constant trickle of letters like this coming into our office, horrendous tales of users wandering around their hard drive, tinkering with files and various settings, and then wondering why all or part of the system won't work. In the case of this reader, what seems to have happened is that he has deleted the HLP file which contained the help for Works.

Help files are a tempting morsel - a quick check on my hard drive produced 44Mb of help files, some of which could probably be erased. But the golden rule is not to tinker with any aspect of your computer unless and until you know what you are doing. People will say that you can't hurt your computer. Not true.

Deleting help files will obviously prevent your having access to them, and you may be able to copy them back from the installation disk - so long as you get them into the right folder - or reinstall the application altogether.

Playing around with other files, especially those with INI, EXE or DLL extensions can cause havoc. If you remove whole folders, you may lose your fonts, the printer drivers or even make Windows unusable altogether.

Tampering with settings can have even more serious effects. One of the benefits of Windows is that it allows you to access and modify many aspects of it, but the down side is that if, for example, you play around with Add/Remove Programs, cache sizes, optimising drives or CD-ROMs, you can end up in all kinds of trouble. For the most part, leave settings alone, as Windows does a fair job of ensuring that your machine runs as efficiently as possible.

This all sounds a bit like Nanny State, but like any complex system, you have to learn to work within your capabilities. No one in their right mind would open the bonnet of a car, say to themselves that those funny rubber-covered wires coming out of that round box thing look untidy, so let's cut them off - but that's precisely the motoring equivalent of tampering with files or settings.

Computing should be fun, so please don't spoil it by acting like a bull in an electronic china shop.

GETTING SENT AWAY

Q I've just discovered how useful the Send To option can be. My question is: Can you add things to Send To? If so, how do you do it?

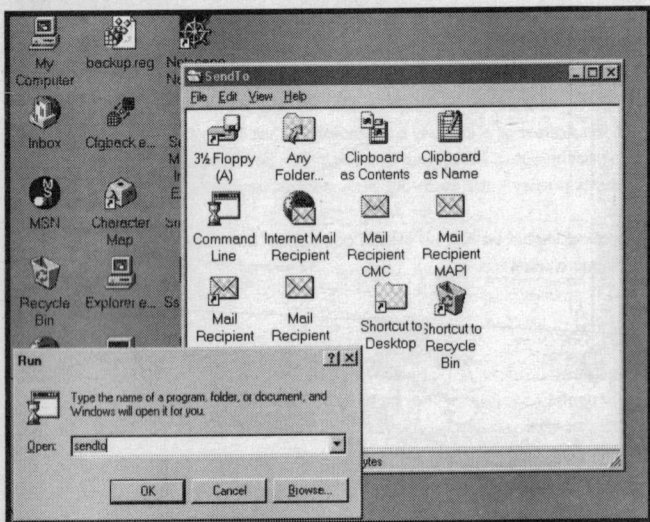

A A word of explanation first: The Send To option appears when you right click on the icon of a file which can make use of it. When you move the mouse pointer over the words Send To, you'll see all the current locations to which you can send (or copy - more about that in a moment) the file to.

Let's take a concrete example. One useful item you could add to the Send To folder is a Shortcut to the Desktop. This is how it's done.

First, click on Start, Run and type Sendto (one word). Up comes the Send To folder. Now we need the Shortcut to the Desktop. Open My Computer, open the Windows folder, locate Desktop and right click on it.

Opt for Create Shortcut. Then right click on the shortcut which appears, and drag it to the Send To folder. Opt for Move here. Now find a file or folder and right click on it. Go for Send To, Desktop, and there you are. Everything is sent to the Desktop almost at the touch of a single button.

Send To is a bit of a puzzle. If you send a file from a folder to the Desktop, it's moved there. Send it back from the Desktop, and it's copied. If you send something from the hard disk to the floppy, it's copied.

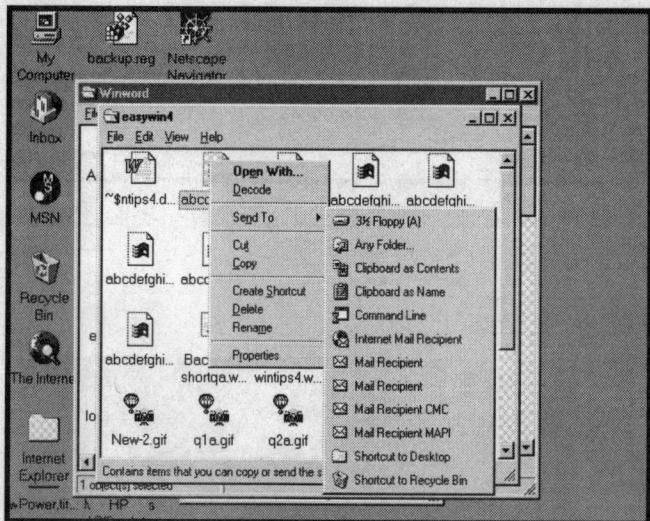

Another useful tip is to add in a Shortcut to the Recycle Bin. This will by-pass the "Are you sure you want to send this to the Recycle Bin?" message. What you do is right click on the Recycle Bin, create a shortcut and move it as described for the Desktop to the Send To folder.

That can really speed up the business of getting rid of unwanted files.

TRAIPSING DOWN THE PATH

Q I like to use MS-DOS Edit, but it is a bit of a nuisance having to type out full path names, or use CD to leap from one folder to another. I bet a friend of mine there isn't an easy way round the problem. Tell me I'm right!

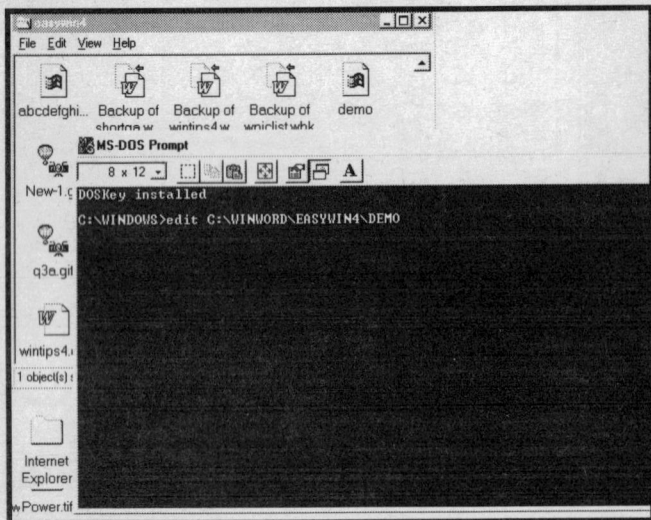

A I hope you don't have a lot of money at stake here, because you are about to lose. Still, you shouldn't be too unhappy, because the tip you are about to get is extremely useful for people who use the MS-DOS prompt. Open a folder which contains a file you want to use the text editor on, then open an MS-DOS Window.

Type EDIT followed by a space. Now here comes the crafty bit. Hold the right mouse button on the icon of the file you want to edit, then drag it to the MS-DOS prompt and let go. The full path name of the file appears by magic, so just press Enter twice (the first time to give the Window focus again) and you are ready to do the editing.

You can also imagine uses for this trick with DIR, CD and quite a few other commands, particularly as it provides the full path, so you can hop from one folder to another in a single leap, regardless of where you happened to be before.

Another way of speeding up your MS-DOS work is to ensure that you have the

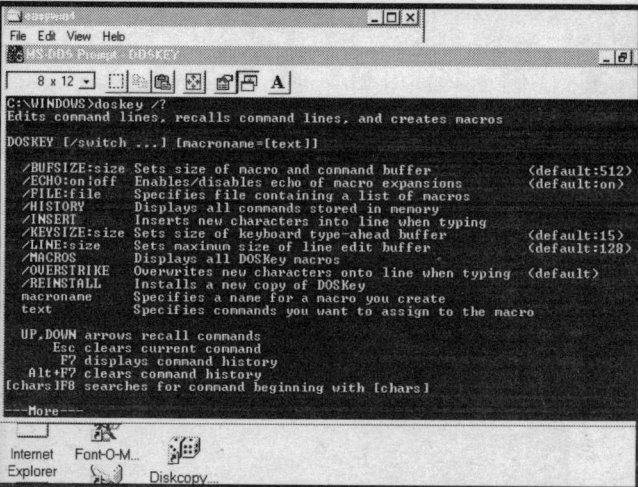

```
                                                       _ |□| x |
File  Edit  View  Help
  MS-DOS Prompt - DOSKEY                                      _ |8|
   8 x 12 ▼  □ ▣ ▦ ▨ ▧ ▣ A

C:\WINDOWS>doskey /?
Edits command lines, recalls command lines, and creates macros

DOSKEY [/switch ...] [macroname=[text]]

  /BUFSIZE:size  Sets size of macro and command buffer     (default:512)
  /ECHO:on|off   Enables/disables echo of macro expansions (default:on)
  /FILE:file     Specifies file containing a list of macros
  /HISTORY       Displays all commands stored in memory
  /INSERT        Inserts new characters into line when typing
  /KEYSIZE:size  Sets size of keyboard type-ahead buffer    (default:15)
  /LINE:size     Sets maximum size of line edit buffer      (default:128)
  /MACROS        Displays all DOSKey macros
  /OVERSTRIKE    Overwrites new characters onto line when typing (default)
  /REINSTALL     Installs a new copy of DOSKey
  macroname      Specifies a name for a macro you create
  text           Specifies commands you want to assign to the macro

  UP,DOWN arrows recall commands
     Esc clears current command
      F7 displays command history
   Alt+F7 clears command history
[chars]F8 searches for command beginning with [chars]

---More---
```

facility called Doskey enabled so that you can cycle through previous commands without having to re-type them. Remember too that Doskey also features a useful command line editor. For information on Doskey, type DOSKEY
/? (don't forget the space before the slash) and, to ensure that it runs every

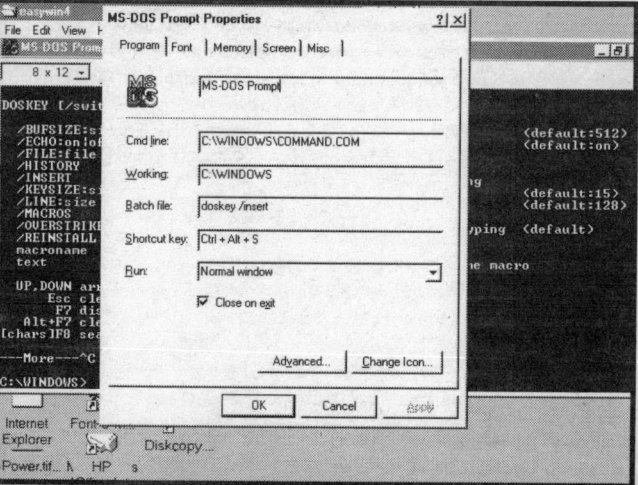

```
  MS-DOS Prompt Properties                              ? | x |

  Program | Font | Memory | Screen | Misc |

   MS
   DS         MS-DOS Prompt

  Cmd line:    C:\WINDOWS\COMMAND.COM
  Working:     C:\WINDOWS
  Batch file:  doskey /insert
  Shortcut key: Ctrl + Alt + S
  Run:         Normal window              ▼
               ☑ Close on exit

                        Advanced...   Change Icon...

               OK        Cancel       Apply
```

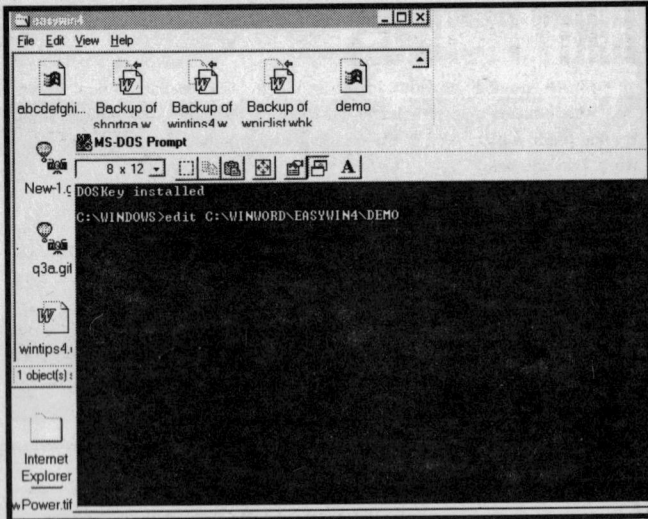

time you open an MS-DOS Window, right click on the icon on the title bar, go for Properties and in the Batch file edit box type:

DOSKEY /INSERT

The Insert is to ensure that Doskey opens in Insert mode. Poor thing, it opens by default in overwrite mode, which can be a real pain.

Finally, you can right click on a folder and open an MS-DOS Window in that folder, which is fine if you just want to inspect or manipulate files in a single folder.

DIRTY PICTURES

Q I have an image problem. I have an image file containing a neat frame which makes a portrait stand out from the page, but, sometimes, when I try and paste a picture on it, the image goes all muddy and I can't get it to work. Can you help?

A At least it isn't the kind of image problem which requires us to tell you to give your anorak to Oxfam and get your beard trimmed. This is a tricky one, but it has to do with the colour depth of the image files you are working with.

If your frame has 256 colours (like a GIF, for example) and you try and super-impose an image with 16 million colours (JPEG or similar), then you will get into bother. The solution is pretty obvious: Don't try and import one image into another if the target image is of a lower colour depth.

INVISIBLE POINTERS

Q When I move the mouse so that the arrow comes over the text it is transformed into a capital I of such slender proportions that it is very difficult to see. Can I do anything about it?

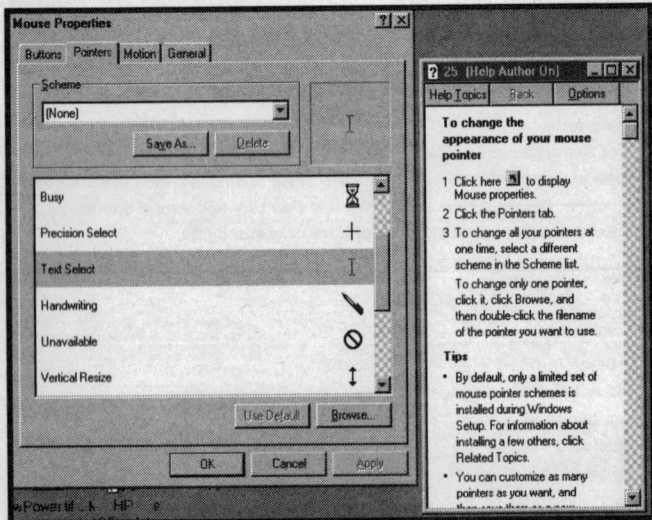

A Indeed you can. The easiest way is to go to Help, type mouse pointer and opt for changing the appearance of the mouse pointer. Alternatively, you can go to the Control Panel and double click on the mouse icon. In the Help panel which appears, you are taken through the operation step-by-step. If you display Mouse properties and click on the Pointers tab, you can see all the pointers in use for the various different modes of mouse operations. Scroll down to the vertical bar which is called Text Select. Now click on Browse, and you should see a list of cursors, among them a couple of alternatives to the vertical bar, one of which is double thickness. Double click on that, then on OK, and you should be in business with a new pointer. Just a reminder, too, for those with sight problems or a poorish quality screen. Go to Mouse properties and click on the Motion tab. Check the mouse trails box and you will find that the hour glass and normal mouse pointers will leave a 'trail' as you move round the screen, making them easier to find.

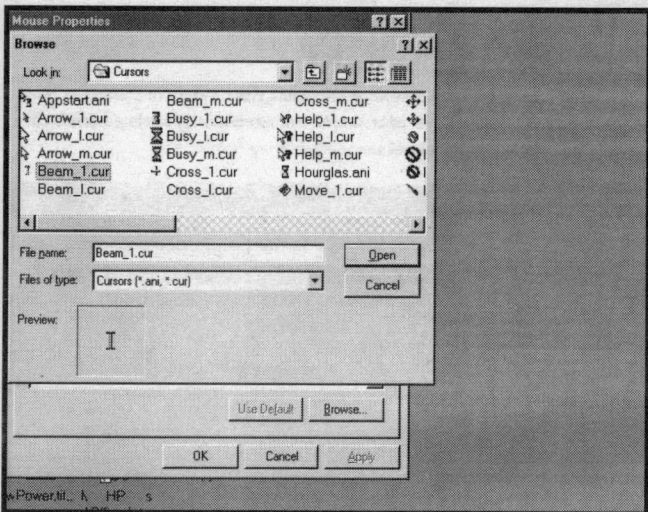

Mouse Properties

Browse

Look in: ⌂ Cursors

Appstart.ani	Beam_m.cur	Cross_m.cur
Arrow_1.cur	Busy_1.cur	Help_1.cur
Arrow_l.cur	Busy_l.cur	Help_l.cur
Arrow_m.cur	Busy_m.cur	Help_m.cur
Beam_1.cur	Cross_1.cur	Hourglas.ani
Beam_l.cur	Cross_l.cur	Move_1.cur

File name: Beam_1.cur   Open

Files of type: Cursors (*.ani, *.cur)   Cancel

Preview: I

Use Default   Browse...

OK   Cancel   Apply

Power.tif...   HP   s

Unfortunately, this doesn't apply to Text Select. To restore the default value, go to the Pointers tab and click on the pointer you want to restore. The Use default button will become enabled and you just click on that to get back to the standard pointer.

RANDOM NUMBERS

Q I have a fairly elderly version of Microsoft Works and I'm secretary of a local darts league. Is there a simple way of randomly sorting names of players for the regular knockout competitions we hold?

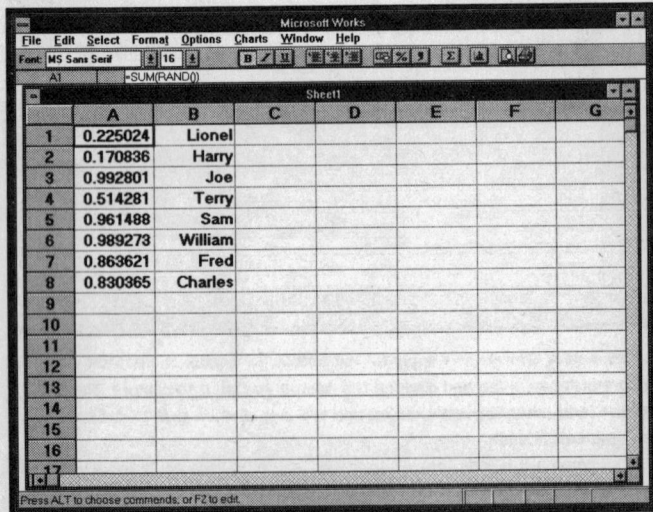

A There is indeed. If you had a more up-to-date spreadsheet, we might be talking macros; but there is a cheap and cheerful way of doing this which should work on any spreadsheet. First of all, assuming you have eight players in the competition (for the sake of simplicity), put their names in column B. It doesn't matter if you put surnames first.

Then in cell A1 type SUM(RAND()) and highlight A1-A8. Use Fill down to put that random number in each of those cells. Highlight columns A and B and go to Select, Sort rows. Opt to sort column A if it isn't highlighted already, and that will sort the random numbers.

If you have manual calculation switched off, the names will be automatically re-scrambled each time you perform the operation. If you have a chart set up for each of the rounds of the competition, just print out the names in the right size to paste on to it.

For a little more sophistication, hide the random numbers, which you do from the Format menu by reducing the width of the column to zero. To unhide it, by

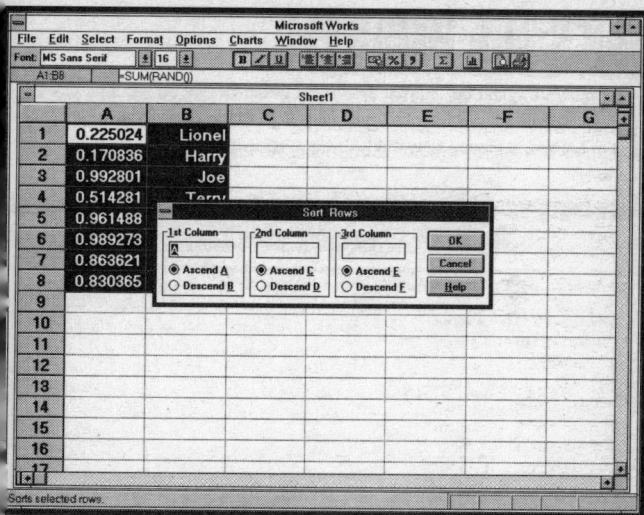

...he way, select Go to from the Select menu, choose column A and then go to ...he Format menu and widen the column. You could also move the names to ...olumn C and add numbers in column B.

...When you select, check that column A is the one selected (it probably won't ...e if the column is hidden), then sort it. Finally, select column B and re-sort ...he numbers in ascending order.

...n case someone is wondering how seeds can be incorporated, assuming you ...ave ranked your seeds in order, sort the non-seeds first then insert the ...eed names in the appropriate part of the draw. If your numbers don't add up ...o 8, 16 or another convenient total, fill up the blanks by calling them byes.

TAB'S THE PROBLEM

Q Someone typed out a price list for me which looked all well and good, but when I converted it to Times New Roman the prices just wouldn't line up. I'm baffled, because they did with the original list. Sample enclosed - can you help?

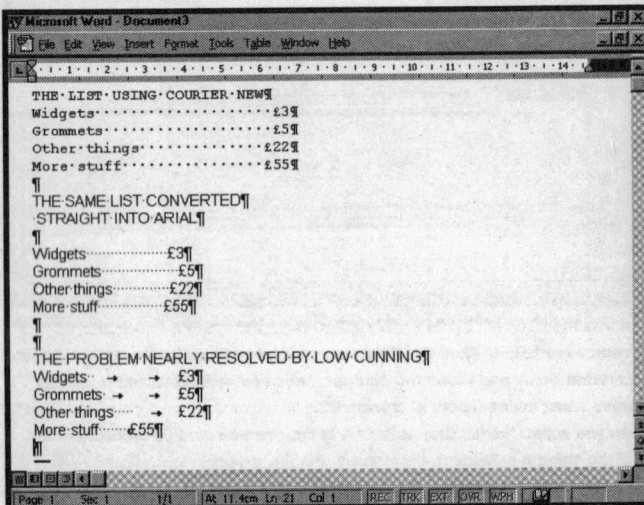

```
 Microsoft Word - Document3                                    _ 8 X
 File  Edit  View  Insert  Format  Tools  Table  Window  Help   _ 8 X
 · 1 · 2 · 3 · 4 · 5 · 6 · 7 · 8 · 9 · 10 · 11 · 12 · 13 · 14 ·

 THE·LIST·USING·COURIER·NEW¶
 Widgets···················£3¶
 Grommets··················£5¶
 Other·things··············£22¶
 More·stuff················£55¶
 ¶
 THE·SAME·LIST·CONVERTED¶
 ·STRAIGHT·INTO·ARIAL¶
 ¶
 Widgets···········£3¶
 Grommets··········£5¶
 Other·things·······£22¶
 More·stuff········£55¶
 ¶
 ¶
 THE·PROBLEM·NEARLY·RESOLVED·BY·LOW·CUNNING¶
 Widgets·    →   £3¶
 Grommets· →   £5¶
 Other·things·····  →   £22¶
 More·stuff·····£55¶
 |¶

 Page 1   Sec 1    1/1    At 11.4cm Ln 21  Col 1     REC TRK EXT OVR WPH
```

A It really is surprising how many people don't use the tab key properly - or at all - and still insist on trying to separate columns using the spacebar. To deal with the problem, we first need a brief history lesson on this topic. Way back in the days of the manual typewriter, every time you pressed a key or the space bar the platen roller (round which the paper is wound) moved to the left by a fixed amount. Whatever letter was pressed had to fit into this predetermined space, so the letter 'i' typically had a long line on the top of it and underneath it to spread it out, whilst the 'm' would look pretty squashed. Then along came the electric typewriter and ever more powerful modern technological solutions to the preparation of documents, and with them came variable spacing, giving the 'i' just the little thin bit of space it needed, and allowing the 'm' room to breathe.

That makes the appearance of documents much more professional and easie to read, but it does mean that you can no longer use spaces as a means of separating out columns - if you want them to be even, that is - because

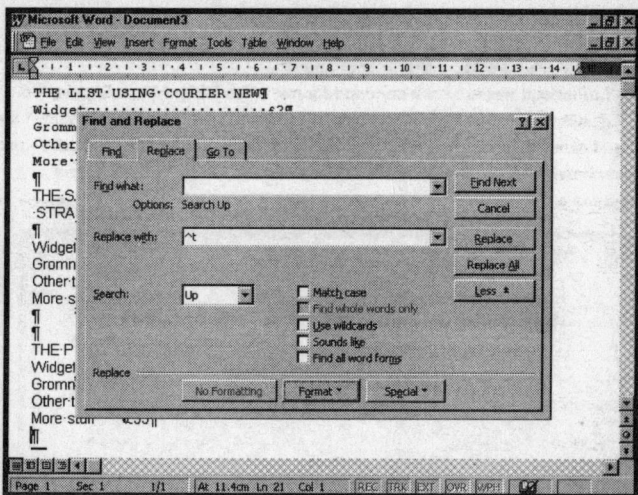

Microsoft Word dialog box screenshot showing:

Microsoft Word - Document3

File Edit View Insert Format Tools Table Window Help

THE·LIST·USING·COURIER·NEW¶

Find and Replace — tabs: Find | Replace | Go To

Find what: (blank)
Options: Search Up

Replace with: ^t

Search: Up

- Match case
- Find whole words only
- Use wildcards
- Sounds like
- Find all word forms

Replace

[No Formatting] [Format *] [Special *]

Buttons: Find Next | Cancel | Replace | Replace All | Less *

Page 1   Sec 1   1/1   At 11.4cm Ln 21 Col 1   REC TRK EXT OVR WPH

---

words made up of variable spaced letters just won't line up properly.
What I guess happened is that whoever typed out the list used Courier, Elite
or some other fixed font from the past, and separated the item from the
price using spaces, assuming that everything would line up properly - which
it does with a fixed space font. Change the font to a variable one, and the
whole thing falls apart.

The first step in repairing the damage is to click on the paragraph sign (¶) on
your Standard toolbar, which will show paragraph marks, spaces and tabs.
Now examine the text, and if there are a lot of spaces, you won't want to go
to the lengths of having to erase them all manually and replace them with
tabs. Here's a really neat trick which will solve the problem - almost - automatically. Go to the end of the price list, and opt for Replace (shortcut:
Alt+E, E). Then type in the Find what box nine spaces (the exact number isn't
critical). In the Replace with box put ^t (the carat sign on Shift 6 followed by
a lower case t - the system won't recognise upper case T as referring to the
tab character). Next comes the important bit.

Click the More button if the dialog box hasn't been expanded and, using the
drop-down menu ensure that the search takes place 'up' the document. Now
press Replace All. What you will find has happened is that most of the
spaces have been replaced by tabs, except for some leading spaces, and
they don't matter. You may find you will have to add an additional tab to level
things out where the unevenness is dramatically large, but, otherwise, that
resolves your problem.

235

SAMPLING THE BABY

Q I thought it would be a nice idea to make a recording of our daughter gurgling, and making general baby noises, and then email it to relatives in New Zealand. I was, however, horrified at the size of the file and implemented Plan B - a cassette recording and snail mail. Is there a way round the size problem?

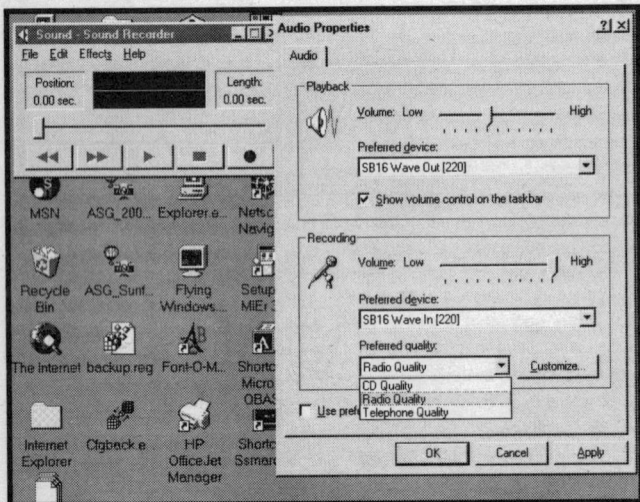

A The explanation lies in the sampling rate, as it's called. Digital sound (or digital anything) depends on taking an instantaneous 'snap shot' of material at predetermined intervals. The shorter the intervals, the higher the quality and the more space the file will gobble up.

In Sound Recorder, opt for Edit, Audio Properties. Now it's up to you to choose your preferred quality. A stereo CD quality sound which takes up over 800K of space can be cut down to a mono radio quality file of 100K. In turn, you can go further down the quality ladder to a telephone file of 50K.

It does sound a bit scratchy, but you may well decide that the best compromise for transmitting a sound file across the Internet is to go for telephone quality. You at least then have the opportunity to transmit material quickly halfway round the world.

THE PROBLEM WITH CARATS...

Q I used the equals sign a few times in a document for a special effect, and then decided I would replace it with the carat character (like a French circumflex), but when I tried to use Replace, I was told that it is not a special character for the Replace With box. Help!

A A nasty little pitfall, this. What you have stumbled across is that the carat sign is used in Word as a prefix for special non-printing characters, so ^t is a tab (as we saw in an earlier answer), ^p a paragraph, and so on. To put one of these characters into either of the boxes click on More if that button is visible, then Special, and then on the item you want to insert. To view the whole lot, go to Help, Find and replace, then opt for examples of special characters. However, that does not solve your problem. There is a standard computing way of dealing with precisely this situation where a particular character has a special function, and that is to double up on the character. So type two carats, and all will be well.

This is similar to the situation in programming languages where a double quote is used as a delimiter for a string literal, and if you want a double quote printed out you have to type two in one after the other.

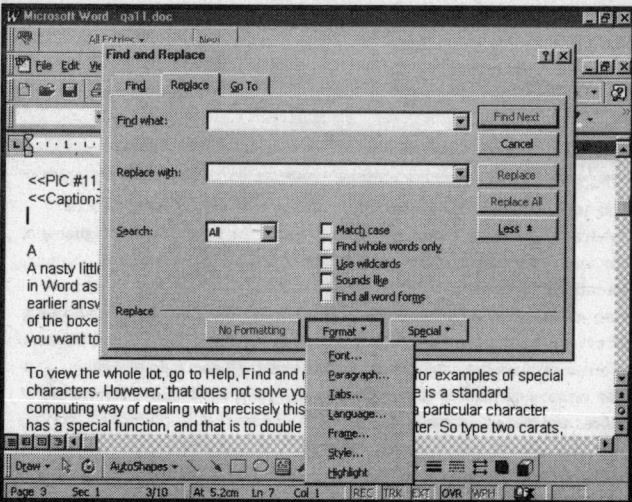

CURSOR QUERIES

Q I know about the hand-shaped cursor on Web page links, but why does the cursor on a Web page change from the normal left pointing arrow to the vertical bar you get when editing a document? Has it got any special value or meaning? And while I'm at it, why are there so many different ways of doing the same thing in Windows? I find it all too confusing.

A You will find that the cursor takes on the 'text select' form, as it is known, when it is hovering over text on the Web page. You can highlight all or some of that text and copy it to the Clipboard for insertion in another application, if you wish.

If your mouse is over text and the 'normal select' mouse pointer is showing, the text has been imported on to the page as an image, for special effect. If you are over an image, right click on it and you will see a pop-up menu. One of the options on offer is to save the image. The trick works in both Internet Explorer and Netscape Navigator.

As for your second question, you should be pleased that there are so many ways of doing the same thing. There are a number of reasons for this. The first is simple choice - use the method you find most convenient in the circumstances. The second reason is that some people prefer to use the keyboard rather than the mouse.

The third reason has to do with the way in which we behave as beginners and then later as more competent users of the computer. Beginners like things spelled out in simple steps, whereas experts tend to want to leap straight in and don't need hand holding.

So, for example, you can switch to bold in Word by going up to the toolbar, locating the B button and clicking on it, going back to the text, typing what you want in bold, then trolling back up to the button and switching bold off. That operation also involves switching from keyboard to mouse and back. The more expert user would probably click Ctrl+B, type the bold text, and then Ctrl+B to return to normal text. Another case in point is launching an application. There are several different ways of doing that - and you may well change the way you work as you become more confident at the computer. It's worthwhile to take time out to review how you work, in order to increase your efficiency and enjoy more what you are doing. Take the Ctrl+B option, for example. You can toggle other text effects, too: Ctrl+I for italics, Ctrl+U for underline. For a complete list, go to Help: Keys, Shortcut keys, Keys for formatting characters and paragraphs.

MINIMISE YOUR TROUBLES

Q I had a help panel open in Word. Then I typed Alt+F, O to open a file. The whole system seemed to freeze and I had to reboot. What was going on?

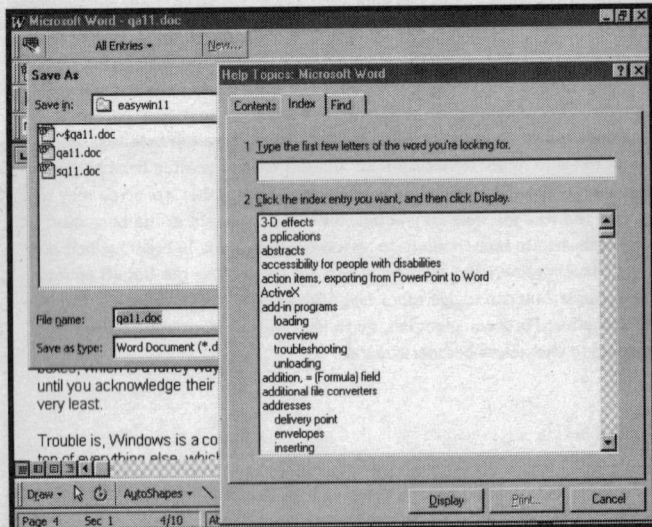

A The system hadn't frozen. This is a situation which can arise from time to time, and the explanation goes like this. Many windows are in the form of modal dialog boxes, which is a fancy way of saying that once they are open, they won't go away until you acknowledge their presence by pressing the OK or Cancel buttons at the very least.

Trouble is, Windows is a complicated beast, and Help panels by default appear on top of everything else, which most of the time is very useful if you are trying to follow advice step-by-step.

However, what happened in your case is that the Open File dialog box did appear, but it was hidden behind the Help panel. You could have progressed quite simply by minimising the Help panel. If you look at the Options menu on Help, you can choose whether or not to have Help on top all the time.

One neat trick which will tell you which modal dialog box is gumming up the works is to try and minimise all Windows, either by right clicking on an empty spot on the Taskbar and selecting the appropriate option, or if you have a Windows keyboard, pressing Win+M.

DOS-WINDOWS DISKCOPY

Q I am a fan of the MS-DOS program Diskcopy, and wonder whether it's possible to run it from a Windows icon on the Desktop rather than from an MS-DOS Window. The real snag, as I see it, is that (a) I am not sure how to put it on the Desktop, and (b) is it possible to add the parameters A: A: to indicate that the copying should be from one disk to another? It's a very neat way to make multiple backups, but can it be ushered forth into the era of Windows?

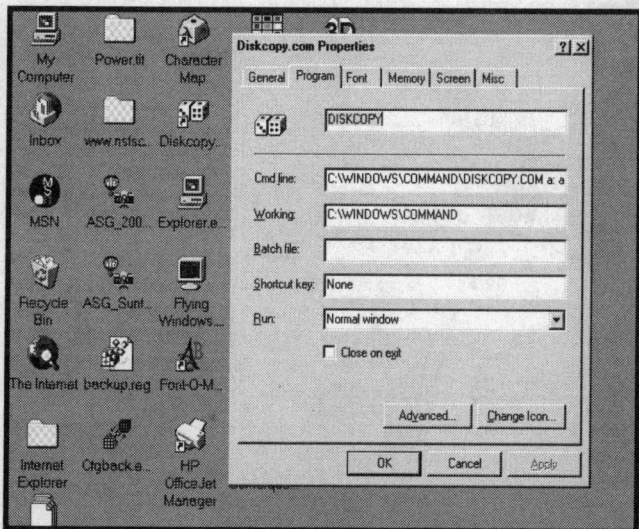

A It is quite possible to perform this little trick, but first just a word to people who may not generally consider using this MS-DOS program at all. You can use My Computer, File, then Copy Disk, but Diskcopy is fine so long as you don't mind taking the trouble to set it up.

What follows is valid for any MS-DOS program. First, find the program, which in this case will be on your hard disk in the DOS folder, which is in the root folder. Open the folder and locate Diskcopy.exe.

Now hold the right mouse button down and drag the icon to the Desktop. Create a shortcut on the Desktop, then right click on the icon and select Properties. Click on the Program tab.

Now add to the end of the command line a space, followed by A: another space and then A: again. Click screen and select window or full screen, depending on your preference. Nearly there.

If you want to change the icon, go to the Program tab again, then click on icons and choose the one which takes your fancy. Now, when you double click on the icon, you will get an MS-DOS window in which you are invited to insert the disk you want to copy from into drive A.

Maybe you don't feel that this is worth the trouble, but if, for example, you have QBASIC and a particular program you still want to run using that language, you can go through the above process adding to the command line the path of the program you want to run with it.

USING VISUAL BASIC

Q I am confused. Now I have Word 97 I see that you can make macros with something called Visual Basic. What happened to WordBasic and can I still use those macros on my new version?

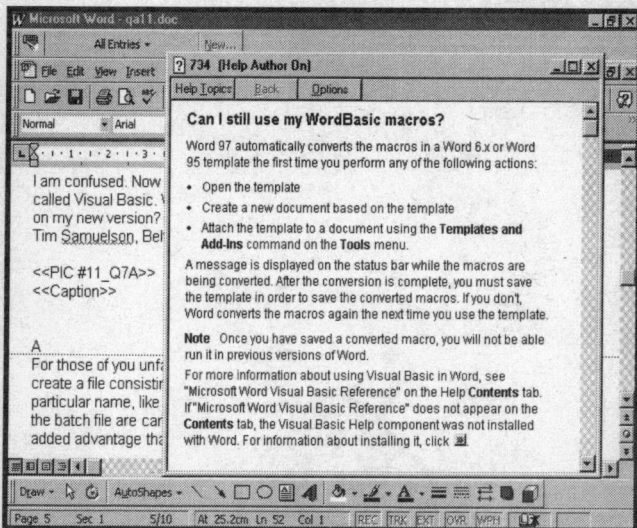

Can I still use my WordBasic macros?

Word 97 automatically converts the macros in a Word 6.x or Word 95 template the first time you perform any of the following actions:

- Open the template
- Create a new document based on the template
- Attach the template to a document using the **Templates and Add-Ins** command on the **Tools** menu.

A message is displayed on the status bar while the macros are being converted. After the conversion is complete, you must save the template in order to save the converted macros. If you don't, Word converts the macros again the next time you use the template.

Note Once you have saved a converted macro, you will not be able run it in previous versions of Word.

For more information about using Visual Basic in Word, see "Microsoft Word Visual Basic Reference" on the Help **Contents** tab. If "Microsoft Word Visual Basic Reference" does not appear on the **Contents** tab, the Visual Basic Help component was not installed with Word. For information about installing it, click ⏏

A For those of you unfamiliar with the term, a macro is like a batch file, wherein you create a file consisting of a series of instructions to the computer, save it with a particular name, like FRED.BAT. Next time you type FRED, the instructions inside the batch file are carried out as if you had typed them in one at a time. There's the added advantage that you can jump back and forward under given conditions, too. One batch file you may well have heard of is AUTOEXEC.BAT which runs automatically when the computer starts up.

The language of batch files was pretty restricted and fiddly to get right. Visual Basic, on the other hand, is a full-blown Windows programming language. Now to your question: WordBasic is the ancestor of Visual Basic, if you like. It is used with earlier versions of Word and has now been replaced by Visual Basic.

What happens when you open a template which contains a macro written in WordBasic is that Word will try and upgrade it to Visual Basic. Check through the macro, and on lines where changes need to be made you'll see the term WordBasic.

A word of warning, though: once converted to Visual Basic, the macros won't make sense to earlier versions of Word; so, if you are working with anyone still using an earlier edition, ensure you keep a version of the template that they can understand.

ROOT DIRECTORY BARRIER

Q I was using the MS-DOS Window to copy files to a floppy, but it packed up at 116 files with the message: Cannot make directory entry. What happened? Was it because it was a long filename?

A No, long filenames are not behind this problem. What has happened is that you have come up against a barrier which applies to all root directories. The root directory, the one which all drives start with, is limited to around 110 entries.

Does that mean you are limited in the number of files you can store on a floppy disk? Fortunately not - the way round the problem is to open a folder in the root directory and save files into that folder. In folders other than the root directory there is no limit to the number of files you can save, unless, of course, you run out of disk space altogether.

VISUAL AWARENESS ON THE WEB

Q How do I make my Web site accessible to a reader with eyesight problems?

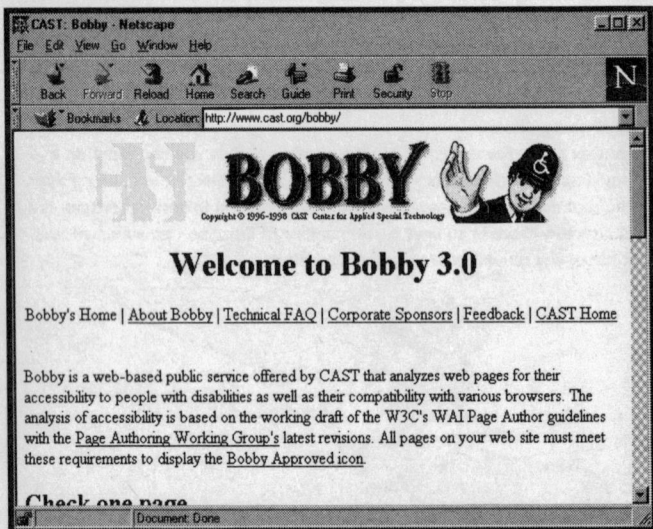

A This is an important issue in these times when people with various disabilities should be given the fullest access to all aspects of life. This doesn't just mean making it easier to get into buildings and on to public transport, but also being able to use modern technology, like the computer. Microsoft has been at the forefront of this drive, as you can see in the Control Panel, where the first icon is Accessibility, which permits people with a wide range of problems to use their machines to the full.

On the Internet, you can help to make your Web site more accessible to visually handicapped users in a number of ways. The first is to ensure that each visual image has alternative text on it. This means that when you put an image on a page using the <IMG> tag, you should add the attribute ALT="an explanation of what the picture is about".

If the image is purely decorative and adds nothing to the content, you should simply put an asterisk into the double quotes after the ALT.

The RNIB Web site editor tells me that frames are a problem for the visually handicapped, as the concept doesn't work for people who read information by ear rather than by sight. However, that can itself pose considerable difficulties for those of us who regard frames a key part of their Web site design. She suggests that, if you need to use frames, you should make your home page frames free and place a link to a text-only version of the site. That in itself is not entirely satisfactory as true accessibility should mean one site for all, not a separate site for the blind.

There is a program on the Internet, called Bobby, which checks sites for accessibility put in place by CAST, the Centre for Applied Special Technology. For more information, go to their Web site at www.cast.org.

ILLEGAL OPERATIONS

Q When loading, my machine sometimes gets as far as showing the wall-paper, then I get a message that 'the program' has performed an illegal operation and will be closed down. Then it freezes and I have to reset the computer. What is going on?

A The problem may be caused by one of the programs which you have asked to load automatically at startup time. The simplest solution is to remove it from the Startup folder. It's a minor inconvenience, but less inconvenient than not being able to get into your computer at all.

The way to do this is to click on the Start button, opt for Settings, Taskbar and then click on the Start Menu Programs tab. At this point, you can either add or remove programs from the Start Menu.

Alternatively, this could just be a spurious error in the system. Windows 95 is so complex that this kind of thing can occur from time to time owing to a rare combination of circumstances.

FIND & REPLACE FORMATTING

Q The other day I wanted to convert a book title which I had underlined into italics. It took quite a while. I am using Word 97. Is there a way of automating the process?

A You don't say how you did it, and I hope you didn't erase the title and retype it. If there were just a few instances you needed to alter, you could highlight the title and either click on the U and B buttons, or press Ctrl+U and Ctrl+B to toggle underline off and bold on.

However, there is a powerful general technique which you can use to find and replace formatting. Opt for Replace (Alt+E, E) and if you see a button marked More, click on that to reveal more buttons (otherwise the full options list will be already open).

One of them is Format. Click on that, and up pops an intimidating list of options. The one you want is the first on the list, Font. You can now either type the title into the Find edit box, or manipulate the font dialog box, which is a bit complicated, so here goes with an explanation.

First, remember that you are now going to set up the formatting you are looking for. Replacement comes later. Now for the options. You can specify one or more of the following: font, font style (bold, italics, normal), size, underline (a variety of options here, the one created by the Underline button or Ctrl+U being single underline), colour, and special effects, like strikethrough or emboss.

Once you have set up the Find side of the exercise, tab to the Replace edit box. You don't have to type in replacement text if you just want to change its formatting. Click on the Format button and select the changes you want. Note that if you have opted for formatting, the No Formatting button becomes enabled, and you can remove all formatting from the search by clicking on it. As you will probably have noticed, formatting choices are listed immediately beneath the Find and Replace edit boxes.

You change them by opting for Format and adjusting the settings. The list of formats requested cannot be directly accessed for fairly obvious reasons. As for the other items on the Format list: you can Find and Replace paragraph settings, tabs, alter language settings, change frames, alter styles and finally highlight the text.

OUT OF THE MS-DOS CLOSET!

Q OK, I may lose brownie points by using the old MS-DOS Editor, but I am rather fond of it. No, I don't have a Reliant Robin and I don't wear a duffel coat, but it's a pretty good workhorse for manipulating HTML files. Problem is, I can't find a way of moving text from one file to another whilst editing, or to and from WordPad and the MS-DOS Editor. Can you help?

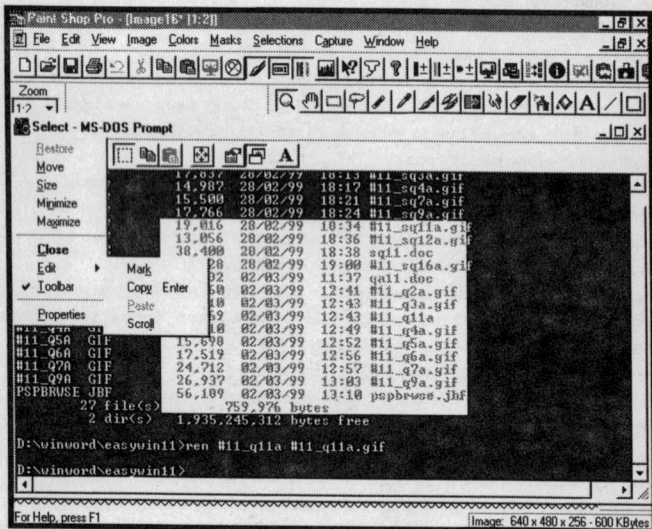

A Join the club of closet MS-DOS users. There are three points to remember here.

The first is that you can open several files at once in an editing session, up to nine, in fact, and you can do so using wildcards. So, if you have nine or less HTML files you can load them by typing EDIT *.HTM. Once loaded, you can swap information between them simply by using copy and paste in the usual way with key combinations or from the Edit menu.

Point two is that you can have more than one MS-DOS Window open at a time, but you cannot use Edit, Copy and Paste to swap information between them. What you need to do is to highlight the text, then copy it to the Clipboard. Now swap to the other open file and click on the Paste icon. You can use that technique to get any text which has been placed on the Clipboard by other applications, including WordPad.

Thirdly, you can also copy text from the MS-DOS Window when it isn't in edit mode, and you can even copy and paste part lines. Click on the icon at the top left-hand side of the top bar, go for Edit, Mark. A blob appears which you can drag across part or all of the screen. Press Enter. The Paste icon retrieves the information from the Clipboard.

Why things are so complicated I do not know, but that's all part of the fun of computing. If it was all easy, we would have no magazine to write, and that would never do.

LOST IN THE SHADOWS

Q How can I achieve text with a drop shadow background? It's an effect which I would very much like to have on my web pages.

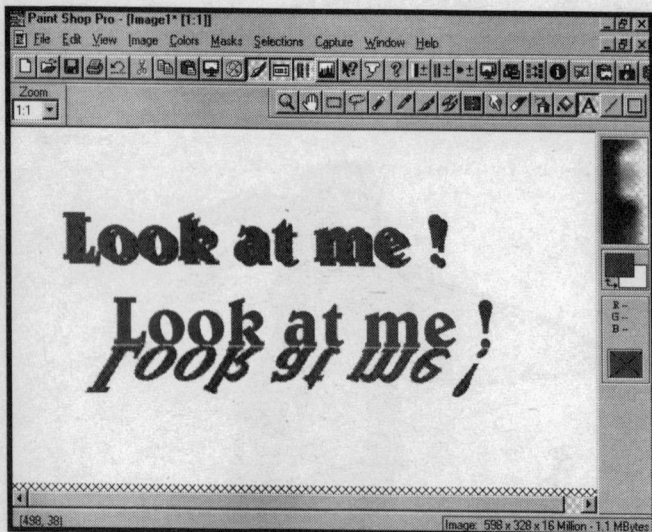

A As you suggest, this is a very powerful way of making text appear striking, especially if you get the mix of colours right. In fact, it is quite easy to do. Let's say you are using a popular graphics package like Paint Shop Pro. First, select your colours for the text and its shadow. Next, make the shadow colour the foreground colour and click on the text tool.

Type in the text you want and place it on your image. Now make the main colour the foreground colour, click on the text tool and use the same text to place it on the image. Now all you have to do is to place the main text on the shadow in such a way that you achieve the desired effect. If your text and its shadow is not in the right place, use the selection tool to cut and paste. On the general subject of adding material to an existing image, you can either use layers (if your version supports this), or simply open a temporary image to act as a working area where you can experiment without damaging the main image. Also remember that if you are working with 16 million colours you can use antialiasing, which smoothes the rough jagged edges you can otherwise get with larger point sizes.

Note that you can also achieve some very striking effects by a combination of techniques. Say you want your text to appear to be standing upright on a plain surface and lit from behind.

First locate the text on the image, and then take the shadow text and use the square selection tool to place a dotted box round it. Go to Image, Flip. The text is now stood on its head. Back to Image again, this time to Deformations and Skew. When the preview window comes up, skew the image horizontally to the extent you want (around 30 degrees is very effective). Then Alt+E to cut it, and Alt+E, T to paste it as a transparent image. Now nudge it up against the bottom of your main text until you have got the two pieces of text touching, and you have created another very powerful image.

LOST & FOUND

Q I like to use Find to search for various things, but I come up against the common problem that everything starts in C\WINDOWS. What can I do if I want to start in my second hard drive (with the letter D:)? Can this be done?

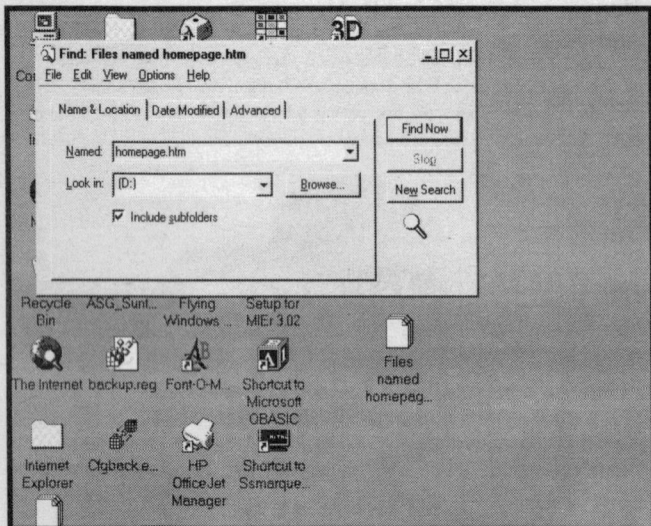

A Actually, it can, and it isn't difficult to set up at all. There are two basic approaches, the first being to ask for the Find to begin in a particular location, the second specifies what you are looking for, starting from that location.

That sounds a bit of a mouthful, but actually it's very simple. Open Find (Start, Find) and click on Files or Folders. Click on the down arrow against the Look in drop down box and find your way to your chosen starting point - or click on the Browse button and use that to get where you want to go. At this point you go to Files and click on Save Search. This places an icon on your Desktop which you simply double click on the next time you want to start a search from that point.

Option two is to specify what you are looking for in the Named window and then go to Files, Save Search. That will leave an icon on the Desktop which will open Find with that search option in the Named window.

WINDOWS MADE EASY SUBSCRIPTIONS FORM

PERSONAL DETAILS

Name: . . . .

Address: . . . .

. . . .**Postcode:** . . . .

Telephone No.: . . . .

Email: . . . .

Signature: . . . .

Date: . . . .

METHOD OF PAYMENT

please indicate your choice of payment method

☐ CHEQUE/POSTAL ORDER (please make payable to Paragon Publishing Ltd.)

☐ CREDIT CARD

Access/Visa/Mastercard/Switch (delete as necessary)

Expiry date:...

Card/Switch number ....

Switch issue number...

☐ UK £36   ☐ Europe £40   ☐ World £46
(12 issues)

Please start my subscription from issue...................

Windows Made Easy Subs, Paragon Publishing Ltd.
FREEPOST (BH1255) Bournemouth BH1 2TA.
No stamp required in the UK. Alternatively, call our credit card line on
01202 200200 (9am – 6pm),
or email subscriptions@paragon.co.uk.

From time to time Paragon Publishing Limited sends out news about exciting new products
and opportunities that are of interest to readers. If you do not wish to receive such   information, please tick this box ☐